On Justifying Democracy

International Library of Philosophy

Editor: Ted Honderich

A Catalogue of books already published in the
International Library of Philosophy
will be found at the end of this volume

On Justifying Democracy

William N. Nelson

ROUTLEDGE & KEGAN PAUL

London, Boston and Henley

First published in 1980
by Routledge & Kegan Paul Ltd
39 Store Street, London WC1E 7DD,
9 Park Street, Boston, Mass. 02108, USA and
Broadway House, Newtown Road,
Henley-on-Thames, Oxon RG9 1EN
Set in IBM Press Roman 10 on 12 pt by
Columns of Reading
and printed in the United States of America

British Library Cataloguing in Publication Data

Nelson, William N

On justifying democracy. – (International library
of philosophy).
1. Democracy
I. Title   II. Series
321.8'01   JC423   80-40732

ISBN 0 7100 0653 5

For my Parents,
Elizabeth W. Nelson and W. Newell Nelson

CONTENTS

Contents

ACKNOWLEDGMENTS

Part of the initial research for this book was supported by two summer grants, a Research Initiation Grant from the University of Houston (1973) and a Summer Stipend from the National Endowment for the Humanities (1975). I am grateful for both grants. I am also grateful to David Lyons and to Donald Lutz, each of whom read a draft of the whole manuscript and offered extensive comments and criticism. Finally, I wish to thank Christine Womack, who typed two complete drafts, and Christine LeMaire, who has typed numerous corrections and revisions in the final draft.

INTRODUCTION

Is there any reason to believe that democracy is an especially good form of government? This is the most important question of democratic theory, and this book is about attempts to answer it. My ultimate aim is to offer a defense of democracy and, in the process, to examine and criticize a number of alternative answers. The constructive and critical parts of the book are not unrelated. The contrast with the theories discussed in the critical sections should illuminate the distinctive features of the positive theory. And the positive theory is designed explicitly to avoid the objections I make to the alternatives.

Theorists trained in a variety of disciplines have contributed to the development of democratic theory. While this book does not purport to be an exhaustive survey of the literature, I do discuss theories that have their origins in a number of different disciplines including economics, political sociology, and moral and political philosophy. Anyone who begins his work in one of these areas neglects work in the others only at his peril. Not only does he run the risk of having his work declared irrelevant by those who start elsewhere, but he is also likely to miss the insights that other work has generated. It is inevitable, and no doubt desirable, that one's work will be in some ways limited by the distinctive perspective of one's own discipline. Still, I hope this book shows a reasonable sensitivity to developments in other areas and I hope it preserves what is worth preserving in the work of those who start elsewhere.

My own training is in analytical moral and political philosophy, and my central concern is with the problem of justification. This explicit emphasis on the problem of justification is what distinguishes this book from much other work on democratic theory. This is not to deny that many writers on democracy have had strong convictions as to its desirability. Indeed, many ostensibly empirical or conceptual debates about the nature of democracy have been motivated by disagreements about what makes democracy desirable. In this book I examine directly the normative assumptions underlying such debates.

SOME METHODOLOGICAL OBSERVATIONS

Any attempt to justify democracy must contend at the beginning with the following problem: A justification (or, more generally, an evaluation) of democracy seems to presuppose an account of what democracy is. But the nature of democratic government is as much a matter of dispute as is its justification. It might appear, then, that we ought to begin by deciding what democracy is. But how are we to do this? I see no reason to believe that there is only one kind of government properly called 'democracy'. Suppose we start with one definition and find democracy, so defined, to be unjustifiable. That does not show that there is no justification for some other form of democracy. Suppose, alternatively, that we find some form of democracy justifiable. It does not follow that we ought to adopt it. Perhaps it is not feasible. Perhaps some other form, or our present form, is even better, but the arguments for it are not apparent when we look at other forms. Where should we begin?

I propose to deal with this problem by concentrating neither on questions of definition nor justification, taken in isolation, but instead on what I shall call *theories* of democracy. Any theory of democracy includes an account of what democracy is, an evaluation of democracy so conceived, and an account of its feasibility. When we focus on the problem of describing and comparing various theories of democracy, not only do we avoid the problem of finding an elusive *essence* of democracy, but we also avoid the tendency to confuse questions of definition and questions of justification or evaluation. I must emphasize, however, that my desire to distinguish these questions by no means implies an indifference to questions of evaluation. I think these are the most important questions. Perhaps *'the* democratic ideal' suggests a unity in the concept of democracy that is not to be found. But there can still be democratic ideals, and the description of *a* democratic ideal is a worthwhile enterprise. My problem, then, the problem of justifying democracy, is the problem of finding a conception of democracy that is sufficiently close to our pretheoretical conception to be of interest, that is feasible, and that can be justified by cogent moral argument.[1]

Some further methodological points are in order here. (1) I do not assume, at the outset, that democracy is a good form of government. For one thing, it seems to me likely that different forms of government can correctly be called democratic, and it is quite possible that these different forms differ significantly in value. Moreover, while our pretheoretical conception of democracy may leave us considerable room to maneuver it does set some limits. I can see no good theoretical reason for assuming at the beginning that some form of government falling within these limits must be a good form of government. (2) I regard democracy as a system for making governmental decisions. 'Democracy' is to be defined in terms of procedures, not in terms of substantive policy. While I think our ordinary use of the term provides some justification for this stipulation, I shall not try to defend it in this way. It is better regarded merely as a simplifying assumption. While there are many legitimate questions to be answered in political philosophy, *one* good question, certainly, is how the various institutions affecting governmental decision-making should be structured. These institutions together constitute what I think of as the government's procedures for making decisions. Their proper structure is the subject of my investigation.

I think it is important, then, that we distinguish questions about what democracy is from questions about its evaluation, and that we distinguish democracy conceived as a type of political decision procedure from democracy conceived as a set of substantive social policies. If I harp on these points, it is because I have noticed a tendency on the part of some theorists, especially those in the social sciences, to confuse, or suppress, some of the issues I want to distinguish. It will be instructive to take a brief look at an example of the kind of confusion of normative and definitional issues that concerns me. For the last three decades, the so called 'revisionists' have set the terms of debate among a substantial number of democratic theorists. They began with the idea that traditional conceptions of democracy (as they understood them) were both conceptually confused and unfeasible in practice. At best, they represent something like an unattainable ideal. The problem was to try to find a *definition* of democracy that was feasible but that also retained as much as possible of the traditional conception, since this conception (so long as it could be freed from confusion) was agreed to

3

be an ideal. Debate has centered, then, on questions of definition and feasibility: theorists debate the proper interpretation of traditional conceptions of democracy, and they debate the limits of the possible. There are pessimists, optimists and pragmatists. The pessimists hold that any conception of democracy sufficiently close to the democratic ideal can never be put into practice. The optimists hold that the limits of possibility are not as narrow as some have thought. The pragmatists, many say, have sold out by adopting a definition that is clearly feasible, because it looks like the status quo, while doggedly insisting that it is still the democratic ideal.

The debate I describe here has generated a great deal of heat, but very little light. The fundamental problem is clearly a moral problem, a problem in normative theory. To what extent, when we depart from traditional conceptions of democracy, are we giving up something of value? Why should we assume that democracy, on a traditional or a revisionist conception, is good? Surely these are the fundamental questions, but they are not the questions theorists ask. I shall, in the end, defend a conception of democracy not radically different from the conception favored by the 'revisionists'. But merely to agree that the system they have in mind is democratic is not thereby to agree that it is justifiable. And, to the extent that they do argue in favor of democracy as they conceive it, their arguments differ from mine.

One final methodological point. Since my major concern is with the problem of justification, my conclusions must be judgments in moral theory. Whether or not democracy, on a certain conception, is justifiable will depend on whether its supposed advantages really are advantages from the perspective of an adequate moral theory. I do not have a complete moral theory of my own to offer. Consequently, both my criticisms of other theories and my defense of my own must be regarded as less than conclusive. That does not make them unimportant. What I try to do is to lay bare the structure of the various theories discussed, and to make explicit any moral assumptions which could plausibly be taken to underlie them. My *evaluation* of a theory, at least for those who do not go along with my normative assumptions, can be regarded as a conditional — 'if we make this assumption about morality . . .'. Indeed, where there are natural alternative assumptions that would alter my conclusion, I try to point them out. The ultimate resolution of the problem of justifying democracy must await further developments in moral theory. But our current ignorance about ultimate matters does not prevent us from saying a lot about which *combinations* of definition and moral principle yield coherent theories of democracy. It does not prevent our saying what types of moral principle could possibly justify democracy, given a certain definition, nor does it prevent us from saying what one is committed to when one adopts a certain moral principle. Again, an example may be helpful.

Many theorists seem to believe that democratic procedures are justified because of some intrinsic feature of those procedures – because they give everyone equal influence, for example, or because they allow citizen participation in decision making. I believe no such facts about democratic procedures are sufficient to justify them. Political procedures affect laws and policies, and these laws and policies can be good or bad, just or unjust. Instead of looking at the intrinsic features of procedures, then, I believe we must focus on the kind of laws or policies the procedure will yield. But all this involves some assumptions about morality of the sort mentioned in the previous paragraph:

1 Laws and policies, not just procedures, can be objectively just or unjust.

2 This justice or injustice is not itself determined solely by the properties of the procedure from which they result. (A just law, for example, is not merely a law produced by such and such a procedure.)

These assumptions are controversial. I fully expect that some will reject them. (I will consider some grounds for rejecting them in Chapter II.) What is crucial, at this stage, is that those who agree and those who disagree make their assumptions explicit. Those who disagree, moreover, must make it explicit which assumption they reject and why they reject it.

ARRANGEMENT OF THE CHAPTERS

I shall begin with a rather short, theoretical chapter in which I discuss some questions about the function of government and about the relation between evaluating governmental structures, evaluating governmental decisions, and explaining the obligation to comply with these decisions. In the following four chapters, I take up four approaches to the justification of democracy which, I shall argue, are all mistaken in various ways and in various degrees. In the concluding two chapters I shall introduce what seems to me a far more promising approach to justification.

This division into chapters suggests a cleaner separation of topics

5

than we will actually find. It represents one possible way, but only one, of dividing up democratic theory. Other divisions cut across these. Also, works which I treat as representatives of one type of theory might sometimes be construed as representatives of other types. Some economic theories, for example, could possibly be interpreted as examples of the types of theory discussed in Chapters II or IV, though I treat them as a distinct type in Chapter V. It is also a bit misleading to say that Chapters II-V are concerned with theories that will be rejected while Chapters VI and VII are concerned with an acceptable theory, since certain notions that I reject when they play a central role in a theory, or when they bear a certain interpretation, nevertheless have some place in the theory I discuss in the final two chapters.

The arrangement of the four critical chapters (Chapters II-V) reflects two themes. First, the theories discussed in the first two of these chapters focus on the *procedures* of democratic decision-making and seek to justify democracy in terms of properties of these procedures. The following two chapters deal with theories emphasizing the legislative outcomes of democratic procedures. Second, the theories discussed in Chapters II-IV, especially those in III and IV, are concerned with the problem of justifying the obligation to obey the law in a democracy as much as with the problem of showing that democracy is otherwise a desirable form of government. Indeed, the theories discussed in III and IV tend to assume that these are the same problem. Thus, in general, we will move from theories emphasizing the problem of political obligation and the intrinsic nature of governmental procedures to theories that leave aside the problem of political obligation and seek a justification in terms of the likelihood of morally acceptable legislation and social policy.

The theory I shall develop in Chapter VI is a theory of this latter type: I seek to justify democracy in terms of its likely consequences. But while this makes my positive views more like those discussed in Chapters IV and V than like those discussed in Chapters II and III, there is also a way in which my own theory is unlike any of the latter four. With the exception of one version of Participation theory (Chapter III), all of the theories covered in these four chapters see democracy as rule by the people, and assume this involves taking people and their preferences, desires or values *as they are*. What makes a system democratic, and what justifies it, is that it takes these preferences and desires into account in governing. Perhaps it sets up a fair competition in which every person has an equal chance of having his desires satisfied, or perhaps it simply gives every preference a chance to be expressed, or perhaps it guarantees that, in some way, every preference will actually influence legislation. By contrast, my own theory does not assume self rule, in any of *these* forms, to be desirable. I argue for a form of representative government, but I argue for it on the ground that it tends to recognize morally justifiable claims and to discourage the expression of morally unjustifiable claim. Thus, a form of democracy tends to produce morally acceptable legislation even on the (undemocratic?) assumption that not all desires are morally entitled to satisfaction. Or so I argue. Even if I am correct, however, this is only a tendency. There is no guarantee that all laws in a well designed representative government will be morally justifiable, and so the problem of political obligation — the *central* problem according to some theorists — still requires discussion. Hence, I turn to that problem in Chapter VII. If a system is justifiable, does it follow that citizens are required to obey its laws? Are citizens required to obey these laws even if some of the laws are not themselves justifiable? The answer to both questions, I suggest, may be 'no'. If this seems surprising, I argue that it at least is not anomalous: even when a particular law is justifiable, it is sometimes morally permissible to disobey it.

I

DECISIONS AND PROCEDURES

When governments make decisions, they take these decisions out of the hands of individuals. What decisions (if any) should governments make, and how should they make them? These are fundamental questions for political philosophy, and they are evidently related. At least it seems reasonable that the choice of a decision procedure should depend on the type of decision to be made. Likewise, if the range of possible procedures is fixed in advance, that may determine which decisions the government can make legitimately. Where do we start? I am concerned here, ultimately, with justifications for democracy, which I regard as a type of procedure for making governmental decisions. If I am right, though, justification of a procedure will depend on the kind of decision to be made. The demonstration that a certain kind of procedure is appropriate, given a specification of the type of decision to be made, is of limited interest for political philosophy unless it is appropriate or legitimate for governments to make that kind of decision. Can we begin by giving an account of the proper function of government?

Suppose we distinguish those decisions affecting no one but the person making the decision from those affecting other persons. Call the former 'self-regarding' and the latter 'other-regarding'.[1] It is controversial whether we are ever justified in taking self-regarding decisions out of the hands of individuals. It is less controversial that some other-regarding decisions may be taken over. When a person's decisions will affect others, there is sometimes a good prima facie case for taking the decision out of his hands. But, to do so effectively requires not only a procedure yielding clear decisions but also power to enforce those decisions coercively. So, a justification for taking some range of decisions

8

out of the hands of individuals is a justification for something like a limited government.

I wish to begin with only minimal assumptions, and I should not want to argue that all other-regarding decisions may be taken out of the hands of individuals.[2] Other people have an interest in many of the decisions we make as individuals, but they are still properly our decisions to make: (1) Some decisions affect others, but only in trivial ways. (2) In some cases the immediate effects of a decision may be significant, but it may take place in a context, like that of the market, which will automatically result in compensating adjustments. (3) In certain situations of interdependence involving coordination problems, individuals care about what other individuals decide to do since the best course of action for each depends on the course of action adopted by others. In many such cases, however, individual preferences are so related that people can be expected to adopt complementary, mutually beneficial plans voluntarily and without outside interference.[3]

While it seems that some other-regarding decisions can perfectly well be left in the hands of individuals, there are some which, it can reasonably be argued, should not be. One case is that in which a decision, if made in a certain way, will result in serious harm for some other person or persons, and in which there is a temptation to make the decision this way. Another case is the case in which people's decisions are interdependent, each stands to benefit significantly if a certain pattern of decisions prevails, but in which independent decision-making would certainly lead to the wrong pattern of decisions. Such cases contrast with the kind of coordination problem discussed in the preceding paragraph, and they play a central role in many traditional arguments for government. Hobbes conceives the state of nature as a situation like this; and the state of nature in Hobbes is very much like the prisoners' dilemma much discussed in modern game theory. The problem of coordinating behavior in pursuit of what economists call public goods is analogous to the prisoners' dilemma.[4] Now, in cases involving potential serious harm or dilemmatic problems of interdependence, there is clearly some reason for people to want decisions taken out of private hands and, perhaps, made by some procedure sensitive to the needs and desires of all involved.

Locke's discussion of some of the 'inconveniences' of his state of nature[5] suggests another interesting class of other-regarding decisions. Locke assumes that individuals in the state of nature will share a moral code specifying certain personal and property rights that people are forbidden to infringe. They will also believe that those who violate someone's rights ought to be punished or to compensate those who are wronged. In the state of nature, however, there will be no agreed upon procedure for deciding guilt or innocence and determining proper punishment or compensation. Since most people are interested in seeing that justice is done, the decision to punish or not is an other-regarding decision; many people have a stake in how that decision is made, and disagreement about the correctness of the decision will lead to further demands for punishment, compensation, and so forth. So, a shared morality and a common desire to see justice done does not suffice for a peaceful social existence. It may have just the opposite effect. A great advantage of government, Locke thinks, is that government provides us with an authoritative procedure for determining guilt or innocence once and for all. Assuming that the procedure is acceptable to all, each will substitute the judgment of the procedure for his own judgment and the disruptive quarrels of the state of nature will cease.

There seem to be three areas, then, in which it would be beneficial to have a central decision procedure to make decisions that might otherwise be made by individuals acting independently. (1) If there is reason to believe that an individual might decide an issue in a way which would lead to serious harm for someone else, there is some reason to take the decision out of his hands. (2) If individual well-being depends on some kind of coordination among persons, but persons deciding on their own would not choose complementary courses of action, it would be desirable to have a central mechanism to make the relevant decisions. (3) If people have a shared conception of how individuals ought to behave, and believe that misbehavior ought to be punished, there are advantages to having a central authority decide guilt and innocence and assign the appropriate penalty. Now, if we were to establish a government to carry out these functions, what would it look like? How might it operate? I have already noted that it would be unable to take decisions out of the hands of individuals unless it was in a position to enforce those decisions; and that would seem to require power to coerce. In its decision-making capacity, as distinct from its executive or enforcement capacity, the government would seem to have two distinct kinds of function, legislative and judicial. How would it discharge these? The government *could* discharge its judicial functions purely on a case by case basis, appealing to the light of nature (and, perhaps, to precedent) in deciding each case that arises. This alone would have certain advantages, so long as most people continued to accept the outcome of the government's procedures, just because it would dispense with questions that would otherwise continue to occupy people's minds and divide them into feuding groups. Things would be better, though, if standards to be used in judging cases were promulgated in advance. If nothing else, it would seem more fair to give people a clear opportunity to plan their lives so as to avoid running foul of the law. In short, if we are to have judicial punishment, we ought also to have promulgated laws.

A government discharging the Lockean function of settling disputes arising within a shared morality, if it is a fair government, will also undertake legislative functions. It will attempt to encode the moral law in positive law. Government will also carry out the first function I have mentioned (preventing harmful actions) by means of legislation. It will prevent decisions harmful to others by taking those decisions out of the hands of individuals, and it will do this by passing laws against certain kinds of conduct. These two kinds of law need not overlap completely. The set of laws designed to make the moral law explicit may not be identical to the set of laws designed to prevent individuals from harming one another. Consider the implications of this. Beginning with the intuitive idea that only other-regarding decisions (and not all of those) could be given over to government, we concluded that, under certain conditions, decisions to punish or exact compensation are properly governmental decisions. But, if we also hold that government should prosecute only violations of promulgated law (and that natural morality is not promulgated in the relevant sense) we may end up with the conclusion that legislation should cover some decisions not other-regarding. We arrive at this conclusion only if morality regulates some decision not other-regarding, but nothing in the argument so far rules this out. There are other problems. So far, when I have spoken of collective decisions, I have had in mind particular decisions made by particular persons at particular times. But laws refer to types of act. Yet it seems clear that there are few, if any, types of decision each instance of which is other-regarding. Thus, even if a government set out to take only other-regarding decisions out of the hands of individuals, it is not clear that it could succeed. Nor is it clear how we could write a constitution that would correctly determine the range of legislative activity on this basis.[6]

I have been attempting to outline some areas of proper governmental authority by specifying some decisions which it would be permissible for a government to make if any decisions were permissible. We have

11

come across some problems. Given some assumptions about how governments have to operate, or about how they ought to operate, it seems to follow that they will almost inevitably engage in activities more extensive than the activities originally specified — even if they are designed not to and intend not to. Moreover, of course, a government, once created, may exceed its proper authority even when it could have avoided doing so. One of its legitimate functions is the enforcement of a prior morality or natural law, but it may fail to capture the spirit of natural law in its legislation, enforce the wrong principles, and violate rights.[7] It may take decisions out of the hands of individuals on the ground that the decisions were likely to be harmful when there was in fact no potential for harm. Finally, it might attempt to promote coordination or cooperation among members of the community in cases in which such coordination is not required for their well being.

The point of giving certain decisions — especially other-regarding decisions — over to government was to prevent certain kinds of harm or to secure certain benefits. But once we have created a government, we have created a new class of potentially harmful other-regarding decisions. We have created a body whose decisions affect people extensively, and whose decisions will not necessarily be good ones. Clearly we do not solve this problem simply by creating *another* decision-making body to take decisions out of the hands of the first. For the same reason that a second level of government will not necessarily improve on the first level, it is always possible that we would be better off without even the first level. This is not to deny that there are also great potential benefits.

Suppose we had a government that limited itself, as much as possible, to the kinds of decision I have discussed here. Would this government therefore be a legitimate government? What does this question mean? Questions about the legitimacy of a government are complex. We might begin by distinguishing the question whether a government has *the right to rule* from the question whether it *rules rightly*. So long as, whatever decisions it makes, it makes the right decisions, it rules rightly. But making the right decisions may be different from having the right to make them. The latter notion connects naturally with much talk about legitimate authority. It is a commonplace that people have something like spheres of authority which others may not enter even when these others would do a better job (would rule rightly). Some of my affairs are *my business*, and you have *no business* intruding unless I authorize you to do so. A government that governs well, in the sense that it *rules rightly*, then, does not necessarily have a *right to rule*. Moreover, the notion of having a right to rule may itself be ambiguous. Having a right to rule may or may not, depending on how it is understood, involve having a right to be obeyed. It may not involve an obligation on the part of others to obey. Thus, for example, a government might have the right to issue commands, and even the right to enforce those commands with threats of punishment, even though the citizens have the right to disobey. Hobbes thought that government and citizens were related in this way, at least with respect to some kinds of commands.[8]

Social contract theorists, I believe, have typically been preoccupied with the right to rule or the obligation to obey. In their view, no matter how well a government rules — no matter how good its decisions — it lacks the right to rule or its citizens lack the obligation to obey unless these citizens have somehow authorized it to rule or consented to its rule.[9] But this is just one substantive theory about the foundation of the right to rule and its relation to ruling rightly. Other theories are obviously possible, including theories that make the right to rule a function of the type of decision that government tends to make, or of the type of procedure it uses. I do not intend, at this point, to propose any substantive theory of legitimacy. My aim for now is twofold. First, I want to emphasize the ambiguity of questions about legitimacy and to stress the importance of the distinction between a government's ruling rightly and its having a right to rule (or to be obeyed). Second, though I do not want to argue that a government limiting itself to the functions described in this chapter is necessarily legitimate, on any interpretation of this notion, I do want to make the more limited claim that such a government is likely to be beneficial for its citizens, at least so long as they mostly go along with its decisions. A government like this is not obviously illegitimate. The functions discussed here are natural and reasonable functions for a government. If someone criticizes a proposed system of government on the ground that it is unlikely to discharge these functions well, it is not obviously appropriate to reply that these are not proper functions for a government in the first place. Anyhow, the governments with which we are familiar do carry out these functions along with others.

The question that will concern me for the rest of this book is the question of the justification of democracy. If we think of democracy as a kind of system for making governmental decisions, the question is whether the democratic system is better than — or at least as good as — any alternative system. What makes one type of system better than another? I have argued that questions about the *legitimacy* of a government are ambiguous: they may concern the quality of legislation or policy, they may concern the right of the government to make decisions or pass laws at all, or they may concern the obligations of citizens to obey those laws. Questions about the *evaluation* of governmental decision procedures are similarly ambiguous. Some theories of democracy focus on questions about the likelihood that democracy will produce good laws. Other theories focus on questions about the obligation (if any) to comply with the results of democratic procedures. These questions are different, but each is interesting. A *complete* theory of democracy should deal with both questions. Any theory of democracy should at least be sensitive to the differences, and recognize that an answer to one question is not necessarily an answer to the other. If it turns out that procedures that are good from one point of view are not good from another, a theory of democracy must decide which questions are the important questions — which aspects of legitimacy are of greater significance.

If we suppose that government undertakes the decision-making responsibilities discussed in this chapter, there is no obvious answer to the question how it should make its decisions. The decisions government makes are difficult ones. Many people will have a stake in these decisions. This is partly because the government is presumed to take over mostly other-regarding decisions, and it is partly because *any* decision, once entrusted to government, becomes an other-regarding decision. More important, not only will many people care about the decisions of government, but most of these decisions will properly be subject to moral evaluation and criticism. Judicial decisions to punish clearly fall into this category. Also, to the extent that the government is concerned to mirror the natural law in positive law — on a Lockean model, to pass laws spelling out the natural laws of property and contract — the government can obviously go wrong morally. There will be problems here, indeed, whether we assume, with Locke, that natural law determines the content of these rules quite precisely, or, with many modern theorists, that laws of property (for example) are morally acceptable so long as they have certain overall distributive tendencies.[10]

Moral principles, on most anyone's theory, determine the proper distribution of rights and duties, benefits and burdens, among persons. Such principles should also govern the interaction of individuals in cases of conflict. But then governments are subject to moral criticism when they adopt policies that lead to the wrong distribution of goods or when they interfere with the rights of individuals in ways inconsistent with moral principles governing interactions. The one area of governmental action discussed here that may seem not to raise moral issues is the area of legislation designed to force cooperation in the pursuit of public benefits. However, even here, it is not clear that the government's actions are not to be assessed by moral criteria. If we look just at the *benefit* side of such governmental action, it may seem that anything government does would be at least permissible. But if we remember that this kind of governmental activity is likely to involve anything from imposition of taxes to conscription, it seems clear that we are faced with problems of distribution involving moral considerations.

If I am right in thinking that governmental decisions typically have a moral dimension, it seems clear that a good governmental decision-procedure must be acceptable from a moral point of view. If we are concerned about the government's 'ruling rightly', a procedure will be acceptable only insofar as it is designed to yield morally correct decisions. (What makes a decision morally correct, however, is a substantive moral question. Does the form of the procedure itself ever confer rightness on its decisions?) If we are concerned with the government's right to rule, or with its right to be obeyed, we might think the question is simply whether citizens have consented to the procedure. But do citizens have any right, morally speaking, to acquiesce in a procedure that may render immoral decisions? Consider the plight of Locke's individuals setting up a procedure for determining guilt or innocence and assigning punishment. They may be better off on the whole if they create an official body to make these decisions and regard its decisions as authoritative. But it is possible (isn't it?) for any imaginable system to err. Can people really give up their right to judge cases for themselves? If not, and if no procedure is guaranteed to render only morally acceptable decisions, then not only can no procedure *guarantee* the legitimacy of a government, but perhaps no system can be legitimate at all. Democrats tend to assume that, somehow, their system has the blessing of morality. But how can an imperfect procedure for making moral decisions have the blessing of morality? The moral status of imperfect decision-making procedures would seem to be very much in doubt.[11]

These questions should lead us to reflect on the ground we have covered. Do the questions government deals with really have a moral

15

dimension? Must they? Are we really justified in having a government? Do we need one? Does it even benefit us? I believe the answer to these questions is 'yes'. One might disagree. The anarchist tradition clearly does on some points. Nevertheless, I shall assume that a government carrying out the functions discussed here is justified and see where that leads us. Assuming a government like this, what reason can we give for the conclusion that it ought to be a democracy? Specifically, what reason can we give in light of the questions raised in this chapter? A justification must take note of the fact that governments make moral decisions, and thus might make them wrongly; and it must deal with the further question whether a democratic government has a moral right to be obeyed. To the extent that a theory cannot solve one of these problems, it should acknowledge it forthrightly. Thus, I shall argue in Chapters VI and VII that democracy is desirable because it tends to 'rule rightly', but I shall also argue that it does not necessarily have a 'right to rule' in the sense that it is always wrong to disobey its laws. What is striking about the theories I shall discuss in the intervening chapters is the extent to which they either ignore one or both of these questions or, alternatively, offer answers which clearly presuppose crucial but unexamined assumptions about the nature or requirements of morality.

II

PROCEDURAL FAIRNESS
AND EQUALITY

Chapter I was devoted to abstract speculation about the function of government and the nature of the decisions governments must make. Governments, I argued, require procedures for making a variety of kinds of decision, and these decisions inevitably affect the moral quality of our lives and institutions. Questions about the legitimacy of governmental decision procedures are ambiguous, but no matter how we understand these questions, it is easy to doubt that *any* procedure will be legitimate. Nevertheless, many people do regard democracy as a legitimate or justifiable procedure, and they offer arguments for this conclusion. Beginning with this chapter I shall shift from general speculation about the nature of government and governmental decisions to consideration of specific types of justification and to even more specific versions of these types offered by particular theorists.

The type of justification I shall discuss in this chapter argues for democracy on the ground that it is a fair or equal political system. I have two reasons for starting here. First, the problem about political systems sketched in the first chapter would seem to be that we cannot trust them to make the right decision. From the perspective of any individual citizen the question is 'why should I give up my power over my life to a procedure that is bound to err?'. Each citizen feels the same way, and so the natural response to the problems I have raised may seem to be a system that gives each person maximum equal power to influence decisions — a fair system. Second, the argument from fairness may seem to represent a natural fall-back position for a number of the other theories I shall discuss in Chapters III-V. Thus, it is worth discussing it first.

17

Of course, there is serious question about the adequacy of the appeal to fairness as a response to the kinds of question raised in Chapter I. If the problem with political systems is that they make the wrong decisions, why are things any better if these systems are fair in themselves? If a procedure results in the wrong decisions should we take any comfort in the fact that each person played an equal part in making those wrong decisions? In any case, is it even true that political democracy is a fair or equal system of government? But now I am getting ahead of myself. Any justification of democracy, I said in the Introduction, should be regarded as part of a theory embodying a definition of democracy and an account of its feasibility. If we set out to defend democracy by arguing that it is a fair or equal social decision procedure, we need to say what we mean by 'democracy', and we need to argue that democracy, so defined, is fair. If we can then show that the kind of fairness in question is relevant to the justification of a system of government and that it is a feasible system, we will have a complete justificatory theory of democracy. Will that approach work?

1 MAJORITY RULE AND FAIRNESS

Suppose we define democracy as a form of majority rule. More precisely, democracy operates on the principle that, for any pair of alternative social states, one is as highly ranked as another just in case the number preferring the former is greater than or equal to the number preferring the latter. (One alternative is more highly ranked than another just in case the number preferring the former is greater than the number preferring the latter.) Now, this is an abstract definition, and there are some serious questions about the practical feasibility of systems fitting this definition.[1] Still, if this kind of system is fair, and the kind of fairness in question is desirable, it would at least seem desirable to implement it so far as possible.

It is evident from the account of democracy offered that it is a decisive[2] rule for making collective choices: for each pair of alternatives it tells us which is socially preferred, or, in case of a tie, that they are socially indifferent. Clearly, also, it is a rule that makes social choice depend on the preferences of the individuals making up the community. But is there any reason for us to believe that majoritarian democracy is a *fair* system of government? Intuitively, it is not the only fair rule for making collective decisions. Consider the following rule: given any pair of alternatives, we arbitrarily assign 'heads' to one, 'tails' to the other, and decide between them by flipping a coin. This rule, I suspect, strikes most of us as fair, though it is not clear how to formulate the conditions of fairness that it satisfies. Presumably, however, these conditions have something to do with the rule's treating persons and alternatives equally. Majority rule satisfies certain formal equality conditions which I shall call, following A. K. Sen,[3] anonymity and neutrality. Anonymity requires that the outcome of an election be unaffected by who votes on which side: each person's vote counts the same, and the outcome depends only on the number of persons voting one way or the other. Neutrality requires that the procedure be neutral among the proposals being voted on. It requires that every proposal have an equal chance of winning. The simple majority rule satisfies both of these conditions. Unlike the coin flipping rule, democracy gives a certain amount of power to individuals by making social choice depend on the preferences of members of the community; but, like the coin flipping rule, it does not give special power to any individual. It distributes power in an equal way.

Some writers on democracy have advocated special majority rules (rules requiring 2/3 majority or unanimity, for example) rather than the simple majority rule. It is interesting to note that special majority rules, as usually understood, fail to satisfy the conditions of fairness I have just discussed. A special majority rule, stated formally, is not a decisive rule: there are some possible arrays of individual preferences over specific alternatives to which such a rule assigns no social choice. In order to make indecisive rules practical they are generally framed in such a way that they give preference to the status quo. (For example, x is preferred to y just in case x is preferred to y by a 2/3 majority *or* x is the status quo.) Special majority rules like this satisfy the condition of anonymity, but they fail to satisfy the condition of neutrality because they assign a special place to the status quo.[4] But, if we are concerned about political equality, it seems reasonable to require not only that each person's vote count the same as that of each other person, but also that each person, regarded as someone with particular proposals to advance, have an equal chance to have his proposals adopted. Granted, in a particular community at a particular time, under either a special or simple majority rule, the chance of each proposal's adoption will depend on the political situation. Still, there is this difference between a special majority rule and a simple majority rule: a special majority rule has a built-in bias for the status quo, whereas the simple majority rule is, as it were, intrinsically neutral.

I do not want to claim that the anonymity and neutrality conditions are definitive of the notion of fairness. Thus, neutrality, as defined by Sen, requires the following: if there are two pairs of alternatives, x and y, z and w, and the pattern of individual preferences regarding x and y, respectively, is just like the pattern of individual preferences regarding z and w, respectively, then either x and z, or y and w should be selected, or x and y should tie and z and w should tie. The coin toss rule I described earlier seems to be a fair rule, yet it does not satisfy the condition of neutrality. Moreover, some philosophers who speak explicitly about the fairness of systems of government seem to use criteria of fairness that involve more than a notion of equality. For example, some people employ a criterion of fairness which seems to entail that a fair procedure must not only treat individuals equally, but must also give them some power over social decisions. (A criterion like this, presumably, would generate a clear preference for democracy over a coin toss rule.) Still it seems reasonable to say that one element in the notion of fairness as applied to social decision rules is a requirement of equality. My aim in this section has been to show that majoritarian democracy does satisfy certain intuitively appealing equality conditions, and to point out that the simple majority rule fairs better in this regard than a kind of special majority rule sometimes advocated.

2 PROCEDURAL FAIRNESS AND JUSTIFICATION

If what I have said so far is correct, there is a sense in which majoritarian democracy, at least in an idealized form, is a fair procedure that treats people equally. Thus, one assumption of the theory under consideration can be defended. But, if democracy is fair, in the sense of the anonymity and neutrality conditions, does it follow that it is a desirable form of government? Does the fairness of democracy justify it?

To some, it might seem just obvious that a fair or equal procedure is to be preferred to one that is not, at least other things being equal. And, indeed, a number of writers do seem to have argued for democracy explicitly on the ground of its fairness, or, at least, to have accepted the relevance of this kind of argument.[5] But is the kind of procedural fairness discussed here in fact relevant? Does it, for example, mitigate the problems about governmental systems discussed in Chapter I?

One writer who develops the argument from fairness in some detail is Peter Singer in his book *Democracy and Disobedience*.[6] Strictly speaking, he argues only that a fair system has a special title to be obeyed, and that does not commit him to the conclusion that a fair system is justifiable in any further respect.[7] Nevertheless, it is worth considering his position at least briefly because he attempts to develop the argument in an intuitively plausible way.

Singer begins his book with a description of three possible kinds of simple society: three common-room associations. One of these associations operates by simple majority rule, and this association, he claims, is legitimate in a way that the others are not. His problem is to offer a plausible explanation for its legitimacy, and his solution is that only this system is fair. But is majority rule fair? According to Singer, majority rule '. . . does divide power equally, in that every member has one vote. . .' (Singer, 29); but he is not convinced that it is therefore fair all things considered. This leads him to distinguish 'absolute fairness' from what he calls 'fairness as a compromise' (Singer, 32). He does not offer a definition of either of these notions, but his examples suggest something like the following: A distribution is absolutely fair if it is the distribution dictated by a complete account of all morally relevant considerations, properly weighted. A distribution is a fair compromise, on the other hand, if it is the distribution people would arrive at as a result of a bargaining process where the parties could not agree on what was absolutely fair but had common interests sufficient to lead them to come to some agreement. A fair compromise 'is limited by what can be achieved in a given situation' (Singer, 32). Now, if, in an association, each person has his own ideas about collective policy and wants his ideas to prevail, then democracy represents the only fair compromise since

> it is only in the [democratic] association that the nature of the decision-procedure makes it possible for everyone to refrain from acting on his own judgment . . . without giving up more than the theoretical minimum which it is essential for everyone to give up in order to achieve the benefits of a peaceful solution of disputes (Singer, 32).

Now, in Section 1, above, I discussed a formal argument for the conclusion that majoritarian democracy satisfies certain precise equality conditions. Subsequently, I questioned whether this kind of formal, procedural equality is relevant to the justification of a governmental decision procedure. Singer offers a different kind of argument for the claim that

21

majority rule is fair, though his argument seems to make use of the kind of procedural equality discussed earlier. (Presumably, it is because majority rule treats people equally that it represents an acceptable compromise.) But Singer's notion of fairness as a compromise may seem to explain *why* procedural fairness is a desirable feature of a political system: Being subject to a political system involves a significant limitation on one's freedom, a significant loss of control over one's life. No such system is justifiable, therefore, unless it would be acceptable to everyone in advance. But only a formally fair or equal system would be acceptable. Only such a system would constitute a fair compromise.

While this argument has some initial plausibility, I believe there are serious difficulties with it. One way to see these difficulties is to consider Singer's own objection to justifications of democracy beginning with a direct appeal to equal rights. If we try to justify democracy on the ground that people are morally equal or have equal rights, don't we need to worry about the possibility that the majority will violate the rights of a minority? 'Equal rights to a cake would not be satisfied if the majority walked off with the whole cake' (Singer, 28). Perhaps Singer's point is something like this: once we start talking about equal rights, it seems natural that we should worry about *substantive* rights, rights other than the right to participate in making political decisions. But, then, there is a similar problem about appeals to fairness or justice: the question whether a political system will yield substantively fair legislation seems *at least* as important as the question whether it is fair taken in isolation.

What is odd about the attempt to justify democracy in terms of its intrinsic fairness, its fairness as a procedure taken in isolation, is that it seems to treat the right to influence political decisions as an end in itself. Yet, on reflection, procedural fairness may seem to be of secondary importance when compared to the substantive fairness of laws or policies.[8] From a moral point of view, what kind of attitude should we adopt toward the choice of decision procedures? In what kinds of situation is the choice of decision procedures a matter of moral importance? Is the fairness of a procedure taken in isolation ever important? There seem to be two kinds of cases worth distinguishing. These correspond to John Rawls's distinction between, on the one hand, perfect/imperfect procedural justice, and, on the other, pure procedural justice.[9] In a case of the former kind, it is possible in principle to describe the kind of outcome we want to achieve — or the kind of decision we want to reach

22

— and the problem is to design a procedure that will achieve the outcome in question. If we can design a procedure guaranteed to achieve this outcome, we have a case of perfect procedural justice. If not, we have a case of imperfect procedural justice. In a case of pure procedural justice, on the other hand, there is no correct outcome specifiable independent of a procedure, but any outcome is said to be fair so long as it results from the operation of a fair procedure.

In situations in which there is no particular correct outcome or independent standard of fairness, but in which it is appropriate to question the fairness of that outcome, we ought to see that the outcome is arrived at by a fair procedure. Such a procedure will guarantee the fairness of the outcome in the sense of pure procedural fairness. But, where there is an independent standard for the correctness of an outcome, the relevant question seems to be whether the procedure is going to produce that outcome (or whether it is as likely as any alternative to do so). Where the independent standard is a standard of non-procedural fairness, or where the fairness (as distinct from the correctness) of the outcome is not in question, it would appear that the fairness of the procedure taken in isolation is of no moral interest at all. That a procedure is fair, in this kind of case, does not count toward its being a good procedure, and that it is unfair does not count against it.

If this classification of situations in which procedures are morally important is exhaustive, it has important consequences for the kind of justification we have been considering. If there are cases of pure procedural justice, then there are some situations in which the intrinsic fairness of a decision procedure may be relevant to its justification. But, an argument based on the notion of pure procedural justice will work only when there is no independent standard in terms of which the procedure's outcomes are to be evaluated. I argued in Chapter I, however, that governmental decisions typically do involve matters of substantive moral principle. The problem about governmental procedures, I suggested there, is that there seems to be no procedure guaranteed to produce the right results. But, the appropriate response to this problem is not to seek a procedure fair in itself — a procedure that distributes decision making power equally. The problem, in Rawls's terms, is a problem of imperfect procedural justice, not a problem of pure procedural justice. It may be true that individuals writing a constitution to govern themselves, knowing that each is fallible, suspecting each other's motives, and so forth, would settle on a system of majority rule as a kind of fair compromise — perhaps partly because democracy satisfies the equality conditions discussed in Section 1. But it is far from clear that this is even relevant to the moral justification of majority rule. If there are independent standards for evaluating legislation, and if the procedure most likely to produce legislation acceptable by these standards is not a fair compromise, then, in fact, we ought to adopt this unfair procedure. This conclusion is unfortunate from a theoretical point of view. It would be nice if we could settle the question of a system's justification by considering only its formal properties, or even just its properties as a functioning procedure, without getting into messy questions about its likely legislative consequences under various sociological conditions. (It is interesting that some proposed reforms of the present system, like reforms designed to assure one person one vote, seem to be defended in terms of an ideal of pure procedural fairness.) However, if I am correct, what we need to do is to deal directly with questions about likely legis-lative consequences.

It is also worth noting, in concluding this section, that some justifi-cations of democracy employing a kind of 'social contract' or prepoliti-cal compromise on a constitution are not subject to the criticisms I have here directed against Singer's argument. What Singer seems to ask is what decision-procedure people would agree to considering only the properties of the procedure itself — whether each person gets an equal vote, for example. A very different kind of justification might begin with individuals choosing among constitutions in terms of their likely legislative consequences, and it might conclude by selecting the consti-tution unanimously preferred. One version of this kind of justification begins with utility maximizing individuals each of whom seeks the system in which he is most likely to prosper.[10] Another version assumes that individuals agree on the correct principles of social justice and then asks what system of government such individuals would, if rational and informed, accept.[11] Now, theories like these are really just picturesque versions of theories which justify systems in terms of their tendency to promote substantive goals like individual welfare or social justice. In my view, these theories approach the problem of justification in the right way, but they require just the kind of messy investigation into legisla-tive consequences that the focus on procedural fairness or equality avoids.

3 POSSIBLE REPLIES AND FURTHER CONSIDERATIONS

Unless we assume that there are no independent substantive principles for evaluating social decisions and that the problem of designing political decision procedures is a problem of pure procedural justice, I have argued, the intrinsic fairness or equality of a democratic procedure is not even relevant to its evaluation as a form of government. While I have taken most of my cues from Singer's book, my arguments, if sound, should apply equally well to other attempts to justify democracy in terms of the intrinsic fairness or equality of its procedures. Unfortunately, my argument has not been conclusive. The question is whether I have ignored some consideration that would make procedural fairness relevant to the moral evaluation of democracy. In this section I shall examine possible replies to my argument. In each case, the reply will be that I have failed to appreciate some aspect of the problem — some fact about politics, or morality, or some distinction in one area or the other. When we look at the problem the right way, it will be argued, we will see that procedural fairness is indeed relevant to the justification of governmental forms. I shall try to show that none of these replies works.

1 In *Anarchy, State and Utopia*, Robert Nozick criticizes 'patterned' conceptions of distributive justice and defends instead an 'historical' theory.[12] The historical theory he defends, which he calls the 'entitlement' theory, says simply that one is entitled to those holdings one has acquired in accordance with principles of justice in acquisition or justice in transfer. Thus, for example, one is entitled to those unowned goods one finds or to those goods one receives as gifts or in exchange for services contracted for.[13]

According to an historical theory like Nozick's justice requires simply that we respect the outcome of a certain kind of process. Yet Nozick's theory is not based on a notion like the notion of pure procedural fairness. He does not attempt to argue that the procedure made up of all the principles in his entitlement theory is a fair procedure and conclude from that that the outcome of its operation is therefore fair. The fundamental notion in Nozick's theory, as its name suggests, is the notion of entitlement; and the paradigm of an entitlement is the kind of entitlement that arises out of a promise or contract. We are entitled to what was promised us, to what we find (if it is unowned), to what we make, and so forth. Each of these principles is a moral principle that stands on its own. The principles that make up the entitlement theory of justice in holdings constitute the set of principles of entitlement like these.

Someone who finds a theory like Nozick's attractive might be led to wonder about my dichotomy between theories concerned with procedures and theories concerned with substantive justice. Nozick's theory of justice in holdings emphasizes processes, and requires that those processes have a certain character, without relying solely on the notion of pure procedural fairness. Why is substantive justice, for Nozick, simply a matter of adhering to the results of certain procedures? Because following those procedures is a matter of acting on independently justifiable moral principles. Hence, an analogous argument for accepting the results of a democratic decision procedure would seem to involve acceptance of some principle like 'whatever the majority prefers is just (or not unjust)'.[14] If we accept a principle like this, we can be concerned simultaneously with the intrinsic properties of the government's decision making procedure and with the substantive correctness of the outcome of that procedure. But surely there is no good reason to accept such a principle.

2 We do not have to be egalitarians, or, indeed, accept any patterned theory at all in order to be concerned about the outcome of a social decision procedure as opposed to its form. A natural rights theorist or a defender of the entitlement theory has equally good reason to be concerned about the procedure's results. However, many people who accept my criticism of theories that seem to ignore the results of democratic procedures will, I suspect, be egalitarians. And some egalitarians may feel that my arguments present them with a problem. They may reason that certain things are intrinsically good in the sense that everyone cares about them for their own sake. It is these intrinsic goods which, other things being equal, ought to be distributed equally. One of these goods, it might be argued, is the right to participate in government; and this right is distributed equally only in a democratic government.[15] Hence, if a democratic government is less likely than some other forms of government to adopt policies resulting in an equal distribution of other intrinsic goods, an egalitarian is forced to decide which goods it is more important to distribute equally.

An egalitarian of the sort I have described here is clearly not compelled to advocate a democratic form of government, since he may decide that an equal distribution of goods other than the right to participate in government is of primary importance. But he must at least hold it regrettable if we have to give up democracy since there is a moral presumption in favor of an equal distribution of the right to vote. When Singer argues that we should distinguish his own theory, based on fairness, from a theory based on equality or equal rights he may have in mind a theory of the sort just outlined. There is nothing in his explicit argument to support this interpretation but his argument seems to lack adequate motivation as it stands. What Singer may want to avoid is (1) a commitment to the general principle that goods ought to be distributed equally, and (2) a commitment to the assertion that the right to vote or participate in government is an intrinsic good for everyone. It is not unreasonable, I believe, to want to avoid these commitments. The second especially seems to me implausible. While it is clear that some people very much enjoy political activity, it is equally clear that many find it thoroughly unpleasant. Still these two assumptions do seem to be assumptions that would justify an emphasis on the fairness or equality of society's decision mechanism taken in isolation. What is interesting about Singer's theory, on the interpretation just suggested, is that he wants to avoid the assumptions while retaining the conclusion. The question I have raised, of course, is whether he can reasonably do so.

3 So far I have said relatively little about the nature of the decisions that social decision mechanisms are supposed to make. Clearly, I have assumed that some of these decisions are going to involve matters of moral concern. If they did not, there would be no possibility of a moral objection to democracy based on its likely legislative consequences. My argument against focusing on the fairness of the procedure taken in isolation takes hold only if we are confronted with a situation in which pure procedural fairness is inadequate to ensure the morality of the outcome. That presupposes that there are independent moral criteria for assessing that outcome.

These observations suggest that we might want to distinguish those collective decisions that involve matters of nonprocedural moral concern from those decisions that do not. The latter decisions will require, it might be said, no more than procedural fairness in the decision making mechanism. It is rather natural, indeed, to interpret certain aspects of the United States Constitution, like the Bill of Rights, as devices to keep basic moral questions out of reach of the electoral process, leaving only morally indifferent matters to be decided by the vote. Even if we reject this, as we surely must, we might think that there are *some* political issues on which morality is silent, and we might think that democracy, because it is fair, is the best procedure for settling these issues. How plausible are these contentions?

Economists and political theorists often distinguish a certain class of goods referred to as *public* or *collective* goods. It is characteristic of such goods that, if they are enjoyed by someone, they are automatically enjoyed by many. It is possible, in the case of such goods, that it may not be worthwhile for a given person to invest in them even though the benefits to all those who would automatically benefit if anyone produced them would far outweigh the total costs of production. The existence of such situations provides a common rationale for organized governmental activity. Private economic decisions, it is said, will under-produce these goods, but the state, being in a position to tax, can see to it that money is invested efficiently.

Let us suppose, for the moment, that this rationale for governmental production of public goods is correct, and let us suppose further that political and economic institutions are so designed that basic moral rights are secure and wealth is distributed as justice requires. Assuming that it is a matter of moral indifference which, if any, additional public goods should be produced, how should society decide among the various possibilities? Is this the place for majoritarian democracy?

The issues here are quite complex. Basically, however, it seems to me far from clear that the situation I have just described is coherent. How is it possible to fix a just distribution of wealth and then, independently, deal with questions about the possible production of discretionary public goods? For one thing, production of these goods will require further taxes, and the combination of these taxes and the production of goods will affect the overall distribution of wealth. Should the new tax burden be distributed in such a way that the pretax and post tax income ratios remain the same? Suppose the collective good in question benefits some more than others. Are we interested in *welfare* ratios or simply in ratios of income after taxes?

I do not have answers to these questions. The important point, however, is that they seem to involve matters of substantive justice or morality. If they are reasonable, then we have not managed to isolate a set of political questions that raise no moral issues other than issues that can be settled by the adoption of fair procedures.

What I have just said assumes that justice requires some fixed distribution of goods or assignment of rights which is capable of being altered by the adoption of public goods legislation. Suppose instead that justice requires merely the establishment of some institution that makes regular transfer payments (like a negative income tax) and otherwise requires only enforcement of some bill of rights and a system of property rules. If this is what justice requires, and if property rights are legitimately alienable, then it is possible to have a system in which people can permissibly seek public goods through the political process. However, a legitimate system for this purpose would have to employ a rule of unanimity, not simple majority rule. The assumption that makes it possible to permit such legislation at all is the assumption of the legitimate alienability of property rights. But if only the possessor of a right can alienate it, then any rule short of unanimity risks injustice. Moreover, even the unanimity rule must be effectively constrained in such a way that it does not result in alteration of background institutions like the transfer mechanism.

John Rawls sketches a proposal like this in *A Theory of Justice* (Sec. 43) though, as his footnotes indicate, he draws heavily on the work of economists like Knut Wicksell and R. A. Musgrave. Once we have secured basic liberties and have established a transfer mechanism, he argues, government should undertake only those further collective projects that achieve unanimous support. More specifically, members of the community are to present complete proposals – proposals specifying production of some collective good together with a tax scheme for financing production at a certain level – and we are to adopt only those proposals that receive unanimous support (Rawls, 1971, 282ff.). Why is the result here supposed to be compatible with justice, and why require unanimity instead of a simple majority? Rawls must assume that basic rights, and taxes and transfers necessary for justice, are effectively immune from revision. He must also assume that justice does not require alterations in these institutions that would be difficult to achieve under a rule of unanimity.[16] Finally, he must assume that justice requires no fixed pattern of distribution. Instead, people are free to buy, sell, trade and give gifts in whatever way they wish.[17] Hence, whatever they decide to do collectively, so long as they decide unanimously, is compatible with justice.[18] But, again, it is important that any changes be *voluntary* changes. That is the reason for the unanimity requirement, and that is why it is not enough merely to require fair procedures. Even in this area in which substantive principles of justice dictate no specific outcome, fair, majoritarian procedures seem to have nothing special to recommend them.

4 I argued, in Chapter I, that we need to distinguish two kinds of question about the legitimacy of a system of government, namely: questions about its desirability or justifiability and questions about the

obligation of its citizens to obey it. So far I have concentrated my attack on the idea that the intrinsic fairness of democracy justifies it, or renders it desirable. Though I have spent a good deal of time on Singer, I have largely ignored the fact that he focuses not on the justification of democracy, but on the question of the obligation to obey the law in a democracy. Is it possible that the intrinsic fairness of a system is relevant to this obligation even though it is not relevant to the system's justification?

For the most part, I shall reserve serious discussion of political obligation until Chapter VII. My remarks here will be brief. To begin, if it is a necessary condition for the existence of a general obligation to obey the law that the legislative system be justified, then my argument throughout the chapter tends to show that the intrinsic fairness of democratic procedures cannot be a sufficient condition for a general obligation to obey the law. I have argued that procedural fairness is not even necessary, much less sufficient, for the system's being justified. Moreover, if it is sufficient for there being a general obligation to obey that the system is a good, or justified, system, then the intrinsic fairness of the system is not necessary. What someone might hold, however, is that there is a general obligation to obey the law, if the law is enacted by a fair procedure, whether or not the political system is justified in other respects. Is there any good reason to take this position?

I have stressed the distinction between a procedure's being fair in itself and its being designed to produce fair or just legislation. An intrinsically fair procedure may well produce unjust laws and policies. How could there be a *moral* obligation to obey the law even when it is unjust? Indeed, even if the procedure is designed to produce just laws, how could there be an obligation when it fails to operate as it is supposed to? These are fundamental questions for political theory. One possible reply, in the spirit of Hobbes, invokes some version of a principle of fairness as formulated recently by H. L. A. Hart and John Rawls.[19] The idea, very roughly, is this. Since we all need some form of central government with decision-making authority, we each have an obligation to abide by the decisions of that authority so long as it satisfies certain conditions of moral acceptability. It is unfair for anyone to accept the benefits derived from a stable system of government without being willing to cooperate; and cooperation here requires that each be willing to comply with the results of the shared procedure for making social decisions.

What conditions must the system satisfy if it is to generate these obligations? Pretty clearly, each person must stand to benefit from the operation of the system, otherwise it wouldn't make sense to demand cooperation from everyone on the ground that each must contribute his fair share to the enterprise that benefits him. Rawls has also argued that the system must be *fair* or *just*. But, if the system is fair, if each stands to benefit, and if certain other conditions are met, then, Rawls says, each person is required to cooperate. Hence, on this view, the fairness of the system is relevant to citizens' having an obligation to obey the law. But all of this, as it stands, is vague. To what kind of 'systems' is this principle supposed to apply? To what extent must people benefit if they are to incur obligations in virtue of these benefits?[20] For our purposes, the important question concerns the respects in which the system must be fair. In the case of the moral obligation to obey the law, there seem to be at least three possibilities. First, we could require merely that the legislative procedure be intrinsically fair. Second, we could require that the system of laws and institutions people are required to respect be fair in the sense that the benefits and burdens of general obedience are distributed properly. Third, we could require that the legislative procedure be fair or just in the sense that it is as likely as possible to yield just laws and policies.

What we are required to follow is some, specific system of laws. It may well be true that we all benefit from compliance with those laws. They may lead us to act in ways that benefit all of us. However, different systems of laws may result in different distributions of various benefits. Whether we have an obligation to comply with the laws, one might argue, will depend on whether the system distributes benefits and burdens justly. If it does not – if, for example, legal and economic institutions systematically favor some groups and not others – then one is not obligated to obey the laws at all. This seems plausible, whether or not the procedures for making laws are intrinsically fair in the sense that each person has an equal vote and each proposal has an equal chance to be adopted or defeated. If this view is correct, it means that we should opt for the second interpretation of the fairness requirement mentioned in the preceding paragraph. In Singer's terms, what is important from the viewpoint of political obligation is that the procedure be a *fairly operating* procedure, not that it be fair in itself.

I do not believe that my argument on this point is conclusive. There are two kinds of situation in which there seems to be a problem about the moral obligation to obey the law. One is the situation in which the law itself, or the system of laws in which it is embedded, is unjust or immoral. The other is the situation in which the person in question opposes the law, whether or not it is actually unjust. In the former case, obedience may be contrary to the requirements of morality; in the latter it seems to compromise the individual's autonomy. Roughly speaking, a concern for objective justice will lead us to stress the former problem and adopt the view that the obligation to obey is contingent on the actual justice of laws and institutions. A concern for individual autonomy, combined with a recognition of the need for some fixed method for making decisions, will lead us to stress the intrinsic fairness of procedures. It will lead us to focus on the question whether each person at least had an equal chance to have his favorite policy adopted. Thus, one question with which we are left is the question to what extent the claims of autonomy should receive recognition in morality. I will have some more to say about this in Chapter IV. For now I simply want to stress that procedural fairness is not obviously the relevant consideration so far as political obligation is concerned.

CONCLUSIONS

I have been concerned, in this chapter, to examine a specific theory of democracy. According to this theory, democratic government is defined as a form of majority rule. Majoritarian democracy is justified on the ground that majority rule is an intrinsically fair procedure for making social decisions. I have discussed the truth of this claim about majority rule, though I have not discussed the feasibility of majoritarian democracy — the question, for example, whether it is possible to establish a system that is, in practice, fair in the way majority rule is in the abstract. I have criticized the theory on the ground that the procedural fairness of a system of government does not justify it. If my argument is correct, it has implications beyond the specific theory discussed here. In subsequent chapters I shall criticize different theories of democracy, but I suspect that the theory discussed here represents a natural fallback position for a number of other theories. That is, if other theories of democracy are shown to be defective on the ground that they embody inadequate justifications of democracy, it will often be tempting to argue that democracy, as defined in the theory, is desirable nevertheless because it is fair. But, if I am right here, this reply will not work.

One final point. It should be clear that my arguments in this chapter presuppose a good deal of substantive moral theory. A reasonable morality, I assume, requires that laws and policies satisfy certain conditions. Procedures for making laws and policies are also subject to moral evaluation, but the standards for evaluating procedures are derivative from the standards for evaluating laws and policies. Morality requires that procedures tend to produce good laws and policies, and good laws and policies are not just any which happen to result from a certain kind of procedure. They must satisfy independent, substantive standards.

Though I have not provided a conclusive defense of these assumptions, I have a clear prima facie advantage over an opponent who rejects them. My opponent is not the skeptic who believes nothing can be justified. He is the theorist who believes democracy *can* be justified by appeal to the fact that its rules are fair in some sense. He believes, perhaps, that people have a right to fair or equal procedures. But it is hard to see how he can believe this without also granting that people have at least some substantive rights – without believing that there are independent standards for evaluating specific laws and policies. Once he grants this, he grants one of my assumptions, and it is hard to see how he can justify ignoring the likely substantive effects of procedures. It is hard to see how he can justify his exclusive emphasis on the intrinsic fairness of procedures.

III

PARTICIPATION

In recent years, a number of political theorists have argued that the notion of political participation should be central to democratic theory. Whether they think the idea of participation essential to the definition of democracy, or essential only to its justification, or to neither, is not always clear. Nor is there agreement among the theorists I have in mind as to what participation involves or why it might be desirable, when they think it is.[1] What I call participation theory here is really a loosely connected set of doctrines, organized around a common core, but capable of being elaborated in a variety of ways. I shall consider some of the possible elaborations here. There may be others, and some aspects of participation theory may emerge in a more favorable light in the context of other theories. But the possibilities I discuss in this chapter are not *mere* possibilities: they represent common ways of looking at democracy.

1 BACKGROUND: SCHUMPETER AND THE REVISIONISTS

Joseph Schumpeter, in *Capitalism, Socialism and Democracy*,[2] effected a basic change in the direction of democratic theory. He offered a characterization of what he dubbed the 'classical theory of democracy', and he argued that this theory rested on a number of unrealistic or unreasonable assumptions. He then suggested an alternative theory which he regarded as more realistic in two respects: first, it avoided undefined (and perhaps undefinable) notions like 'the common good' or 'the will of the people', and, second, it embodied an account of what democracy is which implied that most western countries conventionally called democracies were democracies.

The classical theory, Schumpeter said, asserts that democracy is 'that institutional arrangement for arriving at political decisions [in which] the people itself decide issues through the election of individuals who ... carry out its will.' This institutional arrangement was supposed to result in realization of 'the common good'.[3] Evidently, Schumpeter notes, this theory presupposes that there is such a thing as the people's will for representatives to enact, and it presupposes that this will embodies a correct conception of something that can be called the common good. Clearly, if these presuppositions do not hold, there will *be* no democracies, given the suggested definition. But, even if we were to drop some elements — for example, reference to the common good — from the definition, Schumpeter might hold that, on the theory he is considering, *justification* of democracy still presupposes that the people's will directs us toward the common good. Otherwise who cares about rule by the people?[4] Anyway, however precisely Schumpeter understands the presuppositions here, he wants to deny that the presuppositions hold. In place of the 'classical' doctrine, Schumpeter suggested that we regard democracy as 'that institutional arrangement for arriving at political decisions in which individuals acquire the power to decide by means of a competitive struggle for the people's vote'.[5] There is no assumption, on this view, that the people have a unified will, or that those chosen to govern adopt policies embodying this will. Moreover, there is no assumption that there is a common good, or that people even have a common conception of the good. When contrasted with the classical doctrine, it seems natural to say that this kind of system is not a system in which the people rule. At most, it is a system in which the people choose their rulers, though even this could be misleading, since there is no assumption that all the people concur in their selection of rulers. The rulers are simply those who win some kind of electoral contest.

This definition of democracy, if it is nothing else, is obviously intended to be realistic. There is no question of its feasibility, since it appears to be a reasonable, though abstract and simplified, description of the prevailing system in many western countries. (Note, for example, that nothing is said about the kind of voting system a democracy must have.) It is compatible with great variation in the extent to which citizens participate actively in politics, and in the extent to which elected officials attempt to respond to the wishes of members of the electorate or to exercise leadership from above. The most important thing about this definition, however, is that it or some variant of it seems to have been adopted by a great number of influential social theorists writing in the last two decades. Since the late 1960s, though, theories centered around the definition under discussion have come under attack by a growing number of theorists who argue that the work of Schumpeter's followers has led to a misunderstanding of what democracy is or of what is distinctively good about it. Many of these critics object to what they regard as a too easy tolerance for 'elite' rule, together with a tendency to ignore the importance of widespread political participation in democratic societies. Their positive theory, based on the notion of political participation, is the subject of this chapter.

Here, more than in some other chapters, it is important to reiterate the note of caution I sounded in the first paragraph. I am attempting to characterize a theoretical movement which derives its unity in part from a shared opposition to another theoretical movement. But of course theorists working within both traditions will differ from one another on many questions causing difficult problems of classification. My approach to democratic theory requires that we distinguish questions of definition from questions of evaluation or justification as well as from questions about feasibility conditions. But clearly, theorists may agree that something like Schumpeter's definition of democracy is correct while disagreeing about the conditions under which such a government is either desirable or feasible. Neither the theorists who follow Schumpeter — I shall call them *revisionists*[6] — nor their critics are as careful as they might be to distinguish these aspects of their own theories or those that they criticize. Thus, for example, one wonders whether participation theorists disagree with the revisionist definition of democracy or agree with the definition but disagree about the value of democracy so defined. The difference between these two kinds of disagreement is obscured, of course, when one speaks of a disagreement about the nature of the democratic ideal.

My purposes are analytical rather than historical. I am concerned to understand and evaluate types of theory in the abstract rather than actual theorists or intellectual movements. Still, to the extent that actual theorists hold the kind of theory that I discuss, my conclusions apply to their theories, and I want my analysis to be relevant to contemporary work. Hence I shall begin by looking at some samples of recent criticisms of revisionism and recent work on political participation.

2 PARTICIPATION THEORY

Jack Walker's 'A Critique of the Elitist Theory of Democracy'[7] is typical of a number of papers. The revisionists, he holds, were primarily interested in formulating a realistic — descriptively accurate — account of democracy. As a result, he says, they 'have fundamentally changed the normative significance of democracy, rendering it a more conservative doctrine in the process.'[8] What the revisionists have done is to 'transform a utopian theory into a realistic account of political behavior.'[9] As Walker sees it, his dispute with the revisionists is basically a dispute about matters of definition — about what democracy is. Yet, he evidently assumes, and assumes that the revisionists assume, that democracy is desirable. Hence, he thinks, in adopting a realistic definition of 'democracy', the revisionists commit themselves to a positive evaluation of the status quo while avoiding commitment to the ideal of the classical theorists. Now, of course, the revisionists might well object to this kind of criticism, arguing that their descriptive theory does not *commit* them to these normative conclusions;[10] and I believe they would be correct. Be that as it may, however, taking revisionist theory to be represented by some elaboration of Schumpeter's conception of democracy, what is the alternative that Walker prefers? What he thinks of as the classical theory is not based on the ideas of a popular will and the common good, but rather on the procedures of the town meeting. It asserts that 'public policy should result from extensive, informed discussion and debate. . . . Public officials, acting as agents of the public at large, would then carry out the broad policies decided upon by majority vote in popular assemblies.'[11]

Democracy, as Walker sees it, requires popular rule in a rather strong sense, a sense in which we do not, and, one is tempted to say, cannot have it in modern society. The utopian character of this conception of democracy, however, does not bother Walker. Indeed, his objection to the revisionists' conception of democracy is that it makes democracy too easy to attain.[12] It directs our attention away from the elements of the classical theory that are most important but are also most difficult to attain. Democracy is an ideal, and, if we cannot attain it fully, we can still strive to come as close as possible.

If we take this participatory conception of democracy to be part of a complete theory of democracy we will be left with two basic questions. First, to what extent is it possible to have a democracy as conceived? Second, is this kind of government a desirable form of government? Answers to these two questions pretty clearly presuppose a more complete account of the nature of participatory democracy. One suspects that it may be difficult to find a conception of participatory democracy that is *both* feasible and desirable, but that remains to be seen. It is interesting, though, that there seem to be relatively few recent attempts to develop a positive account of participatory democracy, though there have been a number of critiques of work that deemphasizes participation. One exception is Carole Pateman's *Participation and Democratic Theory*.[13]

Walker takes Schumpeter to be the prototypical revisionist, but his conception of the classical theory of democracy differs from Schumpeter's. Pateman goes a step further: 'What neither its critics or its defenders have realized is that *the notion of a 'classical theory of democracy' is a myth*.'[14] She finds no 'classical' theory that is just like the theory Schumpeter criticized, and, in her examination of traditional theorists, she finds at least two distinct theories that might deserve to be called classical. One of these theories, which she claims to find in the work of Jeremy Bentham and James Mill, has at least something in common with Schumpeter's conception of the classical theory. Both writers, she says, focus on national politics, and both expect the general populace to participate in politics at least to the extent that they vote in elections. Voters are expected to exercise considerable control over their representatives in order to insure the protection of their interests. In doing so, voters see to it that legislation tends toward the common good, since the common good is conceived as the protection and advancement of everyone's interests. In general, then, the people make their will known, and representatives attempt to enact this will. The function of political participation is to protect and advance the interests of the people.[15]

If these 'classical theorists' look something like Schumpeter's, there is another group that does not. The theorists in this second group do stress the importance of widespread political participation, but their primary aim is not a national politics directed to the common good. Their aim, instead, is what Pateman calls 'a participatory society'.[16] They tend to advocate extensive participation in areas other than national politics, and they tend not to seek it merely as a means to external political goals like the protection of economic or personal interests. A participatory society is a society in which an individual is 'able to participate in all the associations with which he is concerned'. It is a society in which 'all political systems have been democratised', and its ultimate goal is a system in which individuals 'exercise the maximum amount of control over their own lives and environment'.[17] According to the participatory theory, which Pateman claims to find in the writings of Rousseau, John Stuart Mill, and G. D. H. Cole, a participatory society is desirable in itself. At least, it is good whether or not it results in national policies directed toward the common good.

3 PROBLEMS AND QUESTIONS

It is worth noting an oddity about the idea that democracy essentially involves participation. If we think of the adjective 'democratic' as a term that applies basically to political systems, as they might be described in a constitution, then it seems odd to include reference to participation in the definition of the term. A specific decision might be democratic or not depending on how many people participated in making it. But, it seems natural to say, whether a system of government is democratic may depend on their being a system of voting, but not on whether people choose to make use of the system. For the theorists of participatory democracy, however, the application of the term 'democratic' to specific decisions or processes of decision-making seems to be the primary one. These decisions or processes are democratic to the extent that there is extensive participation by all those involved. A society is democratic to the extent that decisions in society are made this way. And a government is democratic to the extent that it permits and encourages democratic decision-making throughout society.

While the participation theorists are concerned with democracy primarily as a characteristic of actual processes of decision-making the revisionists are interested in it primarily as a type of national political system. Consequently, we might wonder about the nature of the disagreement between them. It is almost as if they are asking different questions, and therefore quite naturally coming up with different answers. Of course, this is not quite true if the participation theorists would, as I suggest, offer an account of democratic national institutions in terms of their effect on the over-all level of participation in society. Still, even if the two accounts of what *make* national institutions democratic differ, their actual institutional prescriptions might be similar. The kind of representative system most revisionists regard as a paradigm of democracy may well be the best feasible national democratic system from the viewpoint of the participation theorists.[18] But there do seem to be some practical disagreements. These disagreements show up most clearly in the case of revisionist theorists who advocate low levels of participation (or regret high levels) in the name of democracy. For a participation theorist who regards democracy simply as a function of participation, low levels of participation, at least over an extended period of time, are incompatible with democracy. But, if democracy is a function of a number of variables, only one of which is participation, then maintenance of an optimal level of democracy, over the long run, may actually require a low level of participation.[19] Of course there are empirical questions here as well as conceptual ones, since it is not clear whether, or under what conditions, extensive participation might result in a breakdown of democratic institutions. For participation theorists, of course, this question is of great importance, and they are anxious to dispute studies thought to confirm the hypothesis that participatory democracy cannot work. As they see it, the revisionists have been insufficiently critical of these studies largely because their conception of democracy leads them to be uninterested in participation.[20] Theorists like Pateman, on the other hand, take the problem of feasibility seriously. Consequently, she has taken a great interest in studies of functioning participatory systems like those in Yugoslavia.

The question theorists on both sides of this dispute fail to address adequately is the question of the desirability of participation. Obviously, to the extent that we define democracy in terms of participation, a society with little popular participation in decision-making will be an undemocratic society. But will it be a bad society? Will it be a better society if the rate of popular participation increases? Why or why not? Surely these are the important questions. Even if we conceive of democracy in terms of participation and conclude that it is feasible and not self defeating, whether we ought to care about it will depend on our answers to these evaluative questions. And it is not at all clear that participation is of much importance from a moral point of view. The problem here is analogous to the problem I discussed in Chapter II. The question there was whether the intrinsic fairness of a government's decision procedures is even relevant to the evaluation of the system of government employing those procedures. Here I am concerned with the relevance of another feature of a system's *procedures* for making decisions, namely, the extent to which these procedures permit, require or otherwise involve extensive popular participation in decision-making. My arguments in Chapter II should cast some doubt on the relevance of participation, but the topic clearly requires more extensive and thorough discussion. I shall devote the remainder of this chapter to an examination of some of the arguments.

4 SELF GOVERNMENT, CONSENT AND AUTHORIZATION

1 A government is democratic, according to participation theory, to the extent that it permits and encourages participation in decision-making by those affected by the decisions. A society is democratic to the extent that there is such participation. We might say, also, that people govern themselves to the extent that they participate actively in making the decisions affecting them. At least, this will seem like a reasonable thing to say if participation involves genuine power over the decisions.[21] If self government, in this sense, is desirable, then democracy as defined by participation theory is desirable.

The question is whether self government as understood in participation theory is desirable. It is not entirely clear to me that self government in any sense is intrinsically desirable. (I shall discuss this question at greater length in Chapter IV.) But it is at least clear that various things naturally associated with self government are not present in the case of government by participation; and it would appear that among the things lacking are some of the things that make self government seem to be desirable. It is clear, for example, that decisions made with the participation of all those affected will not necessarily be acceptable to all those who participated. Sometimes, widespread participation in the decision-making process may result in a kind of consensus so that decisions will end up being unanimous. In other cases, though, widespread involvement in decision-making may serve to cement and exacerbate differences.[22] In general, widespread involvement in decision-making by no means guarantees that each person will be able to control his own destiny. If that is the purpose of self government, government by participation does not achieve this purpose. It may be true that people who participate in the process of decision-making — especially if this involves extensive, calm and rational discussion with other participants — will come to have a better understanding of the views of those with whom they disagree. They may, as a result, be more willing to acquiesce in decisions with which they do not fully agree; and they may come to *feel* that they are free and in control of their lives. To the extent that this happens, a participatory society will tend to be a *stable* society, and one disagreement between participation theorists and revisionists will be resolved in favor of the former.[23] However, feeling free and being free are different. So also, being in control of one's life and being willing to acquiesce in group decisions are different. Whatever is desirable about self government presumably requires the former, not merely the latter.[24]

2 In the minds of some theorists participation seems to be associated with the idea of self government or government by the people via the additional notion of consent. It is because those who participate in government are thought thereby to consent to governmental acts or authorize their representatives to act that they can be said to be self governing. Moreover, since, in the language of the Declaration of Independence, 'governments derive their just powers from the consent of the governed', participation seems to be relevant to the justification of a government, insofar as participation amounts to a kind of consent. But there are important questions concerning this approach to justification. First, there is the question whether participation does constitute anything like consent or authorization. Second, there is the question whether consent or authorization is relevant to the justification of a system of government, and, if so, how?

If citizens can correctly be said to authorize their elected officials to govern them, there is a fairly clear, if rather legalistic, sense in which they are self governing: elected officials act with the authority of their citizens. They are empowered to act for their citizens as agents, rather as if they had a power of attorney. The longevity of this metaphor for governmental authority – it is prominent in the works of Hobbes[25] – attests to its power. But, in Hobbes, the authorization of the sovereign takes place at the initial constitution of government. It is a one-time occurrence. In much modern democratic theory, authorization is thought to take place with each election. It is not a constitution or form of government that is authorized to act for the citizens, but a series of administrations. By participating in the electoral process, citizens authorize the winner of each election to act in their name. But why should we think that participation authorizes in this way? Why, especially, should we think that those voting on the losing side authorize the winner to govern in their name?

Similar questions obviously arise in connection with the notion of consent. The claim that participants consent to their government seems less relevant to the idea of self government than does the claim that they authorize their government to act for them. The idea of consent connects more directly with the problem of political obligation: insofar as people consent to their government or to their laws, they have an obligation to obey. Consenting is like promising. But to say that they have (something like) a promissory obligation to obey the government is not to say that they are self governing. When it is said that governments derive their just powers from the consent of the governed, what is meant, one suspects, is simply that people are obligated to obey the laws of government only insofar as people have consented to those laws, or to the power exercised in passing those laws. Still, even if the notions of consent and authorization function differently in the justification of governments or of the obligation to obey the law, it is doubtful that political participation constitutes consent for the same reasons that it is doubtful that it constitutes authorization. Why, again, should we think that those who vote on the losing side, just because they bothered to vote at all, have consented to be governed by the winner?

This question is not new. It has troubled theorists for a long time. What is surprising is their persistence in holding that, somehow, participation does constitute consent despite the difficulties with the idea. (Why? Is it assumed that *the* central problem in political theory is the problem of political obligation? Is it assumed that there is no source of obligation other than promising or consent?[26] Why make these assumptions?) In *Democracy and Disobedience*[27] Peter Singer examines again the relation between participation and consent. He agrees that participation in the voting process does not by itself constitute consent to the outcome of the election. He notes that one certainly *could* participate in an election without intending to abide by an unfavorable outcome, and he also notes that there seems to be a problem about the person who participates on the losing side.[28] But, while he claims that there can be participation without consent, he argues nevertheless that participation constitutes a kind of 'quasi-consent', and that this quasi-consent generates obligations like those of consent proper. Singer argues that, in the normal case, participants in a democratic decision process do consent to the outcome of the process, whatever it is. Consequently, the act of participation comes to have the conventional significance of an expression of consent even when actual consent is lacking. Since it has this conventional significance, anyone who participates without expressly avowing his intention to disobey if the outcome is unfavorable thereby gives rise to legitimate expectations on the part of others that he will obey. Thus, he incurs an obligation to accept any outcome.[29]

Singer's assertion that participation must normally involve consent to the outcome of the procedure clearly plays a central role in his argument. Why should we accept it? He argues that there is a 'conceptual' connection between voting and consenting. There would be no point in having the institution of voting − and, I suppose, there would thus be no voting − if people did not normally go along with the outcome of the vote. Assuming this, Singer says, 'the normal case of voting must, because of what voting is, be a case in which there is consent'.[30] I believe this argument is unsound. Singer's idea seems to be that there would be no point in voting (and therefore no voting) if voting did not have an effect − if what happened did not depend in some way on the number of votes cast in an election. This assertion has some plausibility, but it does not entail that there must normally be consent. Suppose that voting typically took place in a highly structured institutional context like that of the state, and suppose that voting usually concerned laws or policies that were to be implemented by the state and enforced by coercive means. In this kind of situation, so long as key governmental officials took themselves to be bound by the results of the vote, it is clear that voting would have an effect even if most people did not take themselves to be consenting to the outcome of the election. They would simply realize that they would be *stuck* with the results of the election, and that they consequently ought to try to influence it. Voting would have a point, even if people took this apparently cynical attitude toward it. Now, it is important to see that this point does not apply only in the case of national elections or elections the outcome of which will be enforced by the police power of the state. It will hold whenever, either because of institutional structures or because of natural facts, the electoral decision can be implemented by the action of only one or two persons. As long as those persons regard themselves as bound by the vote, the vote will have an effect on people, and so there will be a reason for voting. (Consider, for example, an academic department voting on whom to hire. Once the vote is taken, the chairman writes a letter offering the job, the dean approves it, and the vote has had its effect. Implementation of the decision clearly does not depend in any direct way on a general willingness to cooperate.)

Singer's argument seems to be unsound, but that does not preclude the possibility of a different sound argument for the same conclusion. The question is why we should be interested in one. If it were true that participation constituted consent, all that would follow is that those who participate have an obligation to obey the laws or acquiesce in the policies of their government. A government that permitted (and achieved) widespread participation would then be a legitimate government, but *only* in the sense that its citizens (or most of them) were obligated to go along with their government. To say this, however — especially when the source of the obligation is simply consent — is not to say that the government is a good government. It may be true that, if a government is good, then people have an obligation to go along with it. (It also may not be true.) But, the converse surely does not hold. If we want to know whether a system of government is a good system of government, we need to know more than that people are obligated to obey its laws.

One question about government, pretty clearly, is the question where it gets its authority to govern — the question how it comes about that citizens are subject to its authority and have obligations to go along with its decisions. *If* there is reason to say that those who participate in the selection of an administration or in specific decisions on laws thereby consent to that administration or those laws, it would be possible to justify and explain political authority in a participatory democracy. I fail to see how this is a reason for valuing participatory democracy. Indeed, it rather looks like a reason for disapproving of it. Participatory democracy, on this view, is a system that (morally speaking) traps people. The more they participate in the political process, trying to bring about changes in policy, the more deeply they become committed to the system even if their views do not prevail. From a moral point of view, participants lose (or at least limit) their freedom to reject immoral policies. The government, being founded on consent, legitimately exercises authority whether or not it governs well. But why should we want legitimate government if we do not have good government?

5 EQUAL RIGHTS TO PARTICIPATE

It is sometimes said that the members of a community have a fundamental right to have an equal voice in decisions that significantly affect them all.[31] As it stands, this seems rather vague. Still, if something like this assertion were correct, we would have a direct argument for some form of participatory democracy, not only in national political institutions, but also in various other social and economic institutions of the kinds that interest Pateman. What about this general claim of right? It seems to have a number of counter-intuitive consequences. If it is to be defended, it must be shown either that those consequences do not follow from the general principle, or it must be shown that they are acceptable consequences. If we adopt the latter approach, it appears that we will need some pretty strong positive arguments in favor of the basic right to equal participation.

The idea of a basic right to equal participation in common affairs evidently has a ring of intuitive plausibility for many people. But consider its consequences. People make decisions all the time that have significant effects on others. Parents make decisions that affect children; employers make decisions to hire or fire employees, as well as decisions to relocate plants and promote or demote employees; property owners make decisions to use their land in certain ways or to build structures of certain kinds; and individuals select, or fail to select, others as spouses. When people say that all those affected by a decision have a right to an equal voice in making that decision, do they think about cases like these?[32] Should I really have a voice equal, say, to that of my Chairman or Dean in my tenure decision? Its effect on me is hardly trivial, yet it seems clear that it is not my decision to make.

Carl Cohen, who accepts a principle of equal participation like the one I have mentioned, is not entirely insensitive to questions like those I have raised. Indeed, he mentions the problem of decisions within the family, and he qualifies his principle of equal participation saying that people have a right to participate equally when they are equal in *standing* and *concern.*[33] The case of the family is a case in which those affected by a decision lack equal standing, and Cohen regards the claim that property owners have a stronger right to vote on bond issues as a plausible claim in light of inequalities of concern. What has happened to the argument here? We began with the idea that people have equal rights to vote and otherwise participate in political decision-making. In order to justify this idea, we introduced a very general right of people to participate equally in making decisions that affect them all. This very general principle, however, while it is sufficient to justify the right of equal participation in politics, seems to have a great number of counterintuitive consequences. Hence, the principle needs to be qualified drastically if it is to be plausible at all; but, once it is qualified, it is no longer clear that it requires equal participation even in what are ordinarily understood to be governmental affairs. I say it is *not clear* that political equality is required, but of course this depends on how broadly or narrowly we take notions like *concern* and *standing.* In Cohen's discussion, they are left sufficiently vague that we do not know what to conclude. Indeed we do not even know whether what I have called counterintuitive consequences are avoided.

It is possible, I suppose, to take an heroic stance with regard to the general principle requiring equal participation. It is possible to acknowledge that, as we see things presently, employers have a right to make decisions affecting their employees, and property owners have certain exclusive rights concerning the disposition of their property, but claim that this is all wrong just because it violates the basic principle of equal participation. But do we really want to do this? Do we want to rule out the possibility of contractual relationships whereby one person gives up control over certain decisions in return for compensation? Do we want to give up altogether the right of private property (which is, after all, in part the right to gain exclusive right to make certain decisions regarding certain owned items)? Perhaps it is true that these institutions are sometimes abused, and it may be that, under present circumstances, the opportunity to gain the advantages of these institutions is not fairly distributed. But that is no objection to the institutions themselves, and the fact remains that they do have advantages: they allow people, within certain circumscribed areas, to gain a measure of control over their lives. No doubt something like this — control over one's life, or 'self government' — is one of the aims behind the principle of equal participation. Consider this question: would people have more control over their lives if the general right of equal participation were instituted, or are they more in control in the present system in which they are able to gain *complete* control over *some* decisions that particularly concern them? The answer is surely not obvious.

So far I have spoken as if the demand for equal participation stemmed from some kind of demand for self government understood in terms of control over decisions that affect us. If this is the source of demands for participation, it becomes most important to determine the range of effects of specific decisions, and to extend the franchise in such a way as to recognize this range. But there is another source for the demand to participate. It is sometimes held that participation is important not because of the measure of control it gives people over their lives, but because the political life is valuable and enjoyable in itself.[34] People want to take an active part in politics, and so they have a right to do so. As it stands, there are two problems with this argument. (1) That people want something is not, in general, sufficient for the conclusion that they have a right to it. (2) It is not true that everyone wants to play an active role in political decision-making. It could be replied, however, that what is in question is not just what people want, but what is good for them — what they need in order to be fully developed human beings.[35] Even here, however, it is important that we distinguish two claims: (1) that political activity is *one* form of activity in which people can find self realization, and (2) that it is the only way in which they can find self realization. Only if we make the second of these assumptions do we have a reasonable argument for a general right to participate. But why should we accept the assumption? I suspect it is false. (My grandfather was apolitical. He was a scholar, and he was not a stunted human being. Is this evidence that the assumption is false? If not, what would be?)

6 PARTICIPATION AND VIRTUE

According to Carole Pateman, I said earlier, a participatory society is desirable in itself, not for its legislative consequences. But this can be misleading. While the value of a participatory society is not supposed to lie in its effects on legislation or policy, she does think its value lies in some of its other effects. Like many participation theorists, Pateman follows J. S. Mill when he says that one criterion for good government is 'the virtue and intelligence of the human beings composing the community'. The most important aim of government should be 'to promote the virtue and intelligence of the people themselves'.[36] The desirability of a participatory society, as she sees it, derives from its positive effects on the character of members of society. Indeed, one of her reasons for advocating the goal of a participatory society — a society in which all associations are run by participation of their members — is her belief that desirable character traits will develop most readily in smaller associations in which people can become more deeply involved. Participation in national politics is less likely to have the same effects.

It seems to me that considerations of this type are at least relevant to the justification of a system of government. It could be argued, I suppose, that the proper function of government is the regulation of interactions among persons but not the alteration of their character. But it could be replied that governmental forms inevitably have some effect on human character; and, at least to the extent that this is true, the nature of these effects is relevant to the evaluation of governmental forms. Moreover, even if we regard regulation of interactions as the primary concern of government, it seems reasonable to suppose that people's characters will tend to affect the quality of their interactions. My quarrel with this form of participation theory, then, does not concern the type of argument offered, but the details of the argument. Consider, for example, the kind of effects on character on which Pateman focuses. These fall into several groups. First, active participation (especially in small associations or in the work-place) is supposed to lead people to develop a 'responsible' character, to enhance group harmony, develop a sense of cooperation and a sense of community, and to lead to willing acceptance of group decisions. Second, it leads people to feel that they are free, that they are their own master, and to increase their sense of political efficacy (and thus their desire to participate more fully), and it teaches them how to participate effectively. Finally, it leads them to develop active, non-servile characters, democratic or nonauthoritarian personality structures, and it leads them to broaden their horizons and to appreciate the viewpoints and perspectives of others.[37]

The foregoing is not an exhaustive list of all the character traits Pateman mentions, but it is a representative collection. The division into groups is not Pateman's. I add it because it seems to me that different complexes of these character traits are relevant to the task of justification in different ways. Basically, I want to argue that most of the character traits Pateman discusses either are not clearly desirable traits, or are desirable only on the assumption that we have already decided to have a participatory society. Partly because of the limited nature of her aims, and partly because of general features of the justification of political institutions which I shall discuss, the apparent circularity here does not entirely vitiate her argument. Nevertheless, it does mean that the considerations she advances in favor of participatory democracy constitute less than a full, independent justification.

Consider some of the traits Pateman discusses. The traits in the first two groups are, in a way, complementary. The traits in the second group — a sense of efficacy, a feeling of freedom and of being one's own master — are traits that lead people to want to participate more extensively in group decisions. The idea seems to be that participation breeds more participation. Thus, *if* we wish a society in which decisions are fully democratic — in which they are made by participation of those affected — we can be reassured that the process of democratization will tend to be self reinforcing. While the traits collected in the second group have to do with the participatory society's tendency to remain democratic, the traits in the first group have to do with its tendency to remain stable. If Pateman is right about the traits in this group, participation will lead people to acquiesce in group decisions, at least so long as these are made by participatory means. Her conclusions, then, are very different from the conclusions of a number of the revisionist writers who think that increased levels of participation may lead to social instability. Pateman's interest in these questions about stability and the level of participation clearly derives from her concern to answer the revisionists' charge that participation may endanger stability as well as their claim that political apathy is simply natural for people. Her general argument, I think, is that increased participation and stable democracy are *both* possible so long as we democratize the *whole* society instead of just national political institutions. Now, I am neither competent to answer the empirical questions here nor particularly interested in them. Even if a stable, participatory society is possible, my question is why we should try to bring it about?

The third group of character traits to which Pateman refers may seem to provide an answer to my question. Nonauthoritarian personality structures, nonservile characters and the ability to appreciate the viewpoint of others may well seem like intrinsically good traits. This depends, of course, on just how we understand these phrases. For example, if a nonauthoritarian is (in part) someone who tends to acquiesce in majority decisions, no matter how outrageous, it seems to me undesirable. (This problem of interpretation figures in a number of questions here. For example, I took a 'sense of community' to be relevant primarily to a willingness to go along with community decisions, but Pateman may think of it in other ways too.) At the very least, the desirability of many of the traits Pateman mentions seems to depend on the assumption that we have a democratic society. Thus, the ability to appreciate the viewpoints and needs of others will at least be more important in a democratic, participatory society than it will be in other kinds of society. This does not make it irrelevant to the justification of a participatory society, but it does suggest that Pateman is not sufficiently aware of the complexity of the justificatory task she faces.[38] Ultimately, it seems to me, we need a reasonably well articulated moral theory. Given such a theory, it would be interesting to know whether a particular kind of political system would produce intrinsically good character structures, as defined by such a theory. But the relation between character, morality and institutions is likely to be more complex than that. Presumably, a moral theory will both lay down certain standards that laws or policies are supposed to meet and offer an account of human virtue and human good. Now, if the political system were so designed that it would produce the right laws or policies no matter what people were like, the effects of the institutions on their character would be important only insofar as the morality directly implied specific standards for judging character. It is likely, however, that the effect of institutions on legislation would depend in part on the character of people occupying institutional positions. Hence, in most cases, the evaluation of the institutions would depend in part on the effect of those institutions on people's character. Roughly, we want institutions that will affect people in such a way that such people, operating those institutions, will produce the most nearly ideal laws and policies. John Stuart Mill, I think, sees the relation between institutional choice and individual character in just this way.[39] He does evaluate institutions in part by their effects on character, but a moral theory — utilitarianism — serves as the foundation of the argument. Without such a foundation, the argument would be radically incomplete. It would rest, as does Pateman's argument, on a merely conventional list of vaguely specified 'democratic' character traits. We need to go further than that.

CONCLUSIONS

I have described a number of aspects of participation theory in this chapter, but I have focused critical attention on the question of the *desirability* of participatory democracy. There seem to be a number of initially plausible arguments in favor of maximizing participation — arguments connecting participation with self government, for example, or arguments connecting participation with legitimate government via the notion of consent. I have tried to show, however, that these arguments simply do not work. A more plausible form of argument would justify the idea of participation on the ground that participatory government would tend to promote character traits good in themselves or traits good because they would result in a well run government as defined by a plausible normative theory. My defense of a form of democracy in Chapter VI will employ an argument analogous to this latter one: I shall argue that democratic institutions promote attitudes in citizens which will in turn lead them to govern themselves in ways consistent with the requirements of morality. And it is possible though this requires empirical support, that participatory institutions of various sorts would foster the same attitudes. In any case, a defense of democracy or of participation, along these lines, can be carried out only within the context of a theory of morality. The participation theorists have failed to provide us with such a theory, and their arguments are therefore radically incomplete.

IV

POPULAR SOVEREIGNTY

Democracy is naturally characterized as the form of government in which the people rule. This characterization of democracy is closely associated with a kind of justification of democracy, for it is often held that the people in a society ought to rule or ought to be self governing. One might, of course, object either to this way of describing democracy or to this way of justifying it. (I shall discuss the latter later on in the chapter.) But it seems to me that the main question facing a theory of democracy built around this characterization is the question of feasibility. Is it *possible* to have a political system in which the people are genuinely self governing? What does it mean to say that the people rule or that the people are self governing? Can we find an answer to this question that will even allow us to make sense of the claim that the people rule?

We must distinguish the question here from other questions with which it is easily confused. The claim that the people should (or do) rule might be understood as the claim that the people should (or do) participate in the process of government in some way. We have discussed the notion of political participation as it has functioned in some theories of democracy in Chapter III. If we require that the people ought to participate in government, we are left with questions about what participation should involve, and with questions about who should have the opportunity to participate – who is to count as the people. But when I ask in this chapter what 'the people rule' means, I do not mean to be asking these questions about the nature of political participation or about the proper extent of the suffrage.

When I speak, in this chapter, of the claim that the people rule, I have in mind the claim that, roughly, the people's choices, preferences or values are reflected in laws and governmental policy. To say that the people are self governing is to say that what they believe ought to be done by the state is done. (In principle, of course, a government could be democratic in this sense without having any of the institutions normally regarded as democratic. The only requirement is that law makers *somehow* manage to respond to changes in the preferences or values of the citizens.)

Unfortunately, it is far from easy to say clearly or precisely what is involved in governmental policy's reflecting the values of preferences of citizens. The picture is this: we examine the choices or preferences of individual members of society, and thereby discover what the people prefer. The government is so designed that its laws and policies automatically reflect the people's preference. But, of course, when we look at the preferences of the people, what we find is only individual people, usually people with *different* preferences. To say that we must ascertain the *will of the people* does not help, for, again, what we have, typically, is a number of different people with different, and sometimes conflicting, wills. Of course, sometimes, on some issues, there will be unanimity. But when it is said that democracy is a system in which the people rule, this presumably does not mean merely that legislation reflects the people's unanimous will *when there happens to be one*. It means that all the laws and policies accord with the will of the people. Otherwise what would be the status of those many laws in a democracy on which there was no consensus? What about the claim that democracy is in general a good form of government?

It is tempting to conclude simply that there is no such thing as the will of the people – or, at least, that there is almost never such a will – and therefore that the theory of democracy we are considering here must be rejected. But this is unlikely to satisfy. It would be too quick.[1] True, if the theory of popular sovereignty is to be successful, we do need to find a coherent account of what is meant by 'the will of the people', and we also need to find an argument to show that state action ought to accord with the will of the people so conceived. But it is not yet clear that this cannot be done. Granted, there is often widespread disagreement among the members of a society, but we do not know till we have tried whether we can find order within this apparent diversity. We will not always find unanimity, but perhaps we will be able to find some way of amalgamating individual preferences and values that will allow us to identify, on every issue, some policy alternative that bears a unique relation to those preferences. If that relation is of a certain sort, we might find that an alternative bearing this relation to individual preferences could plausibly be called the will of the people and that it is of moral interest.

The organization of the following discussion requires some explanation. My aim is to present a sympathetic account of a theory of democracy built around the notion of popular sovereignty. Thus, first, I consider the problem of giving content to the notion of the will of the people, and I conclude that it is not clearly impossible. Second, I consider some strong arguments for the importance of popular sovereignty. Up to this point, the theory of popular sovereignty looks at least plausible. A complete theory, however, requires a conception of the will of the people that fits in the right way with the argument for its importance. It is this problem that stands in the way of a complete theory. With that in mind, I turn to a reconsideration of the arguments for the importance of popular sovereignty and argue that these arguments, though initially plausible, cannot ultimately be accepted.

The organization I have just outlined is prompted by my desire to treat the various results discussed in this chapter as parts of a single more or less unified theory. As it happens, some of these results, like Arrow's theorem, have also been thought relevant to the theory of democracy in other ways. Rather than interrupt the main flow of the argument, however, I have added an appendix to this chapter in which I discuss briefly the theory of representation and the reasonableness of majority voting procedures in light of the results outlined in the rest of the chapter.

1 ARROW'S THEOREM

It is in the context of this kind of theory, I believe, that Kenneth Arrow's widely discussed 'impossibility theorem'[2] becomes relevant to democratic theory. I wish to discuss Arrow's theorem here in some detail (though informally) for two reasons. First, I think it provides us with an instructive example of the kinds of problems we will encounter in attempting to give an account of 'the will of the people'. Second, it is easy to think that Arrow's theorem has more significance for democratic theory than it does have. Briefly, as I read Arrow, the main motive behind his unsuccessful attempt to find a social welfare function is a desire to explicate a notion very like the notion of the will of the people.[3] While his results also raise certain questions about social decision procedures — like voting procedures — he certainly does not show that no such procedure is ever rational or reasonable.[4] Arrow's result does tend to undermine a theory of democracy based on democracy's claim to govern according to the will of the people, but it does not show that democracy has nothing to recommend it. Arrow's theorem shows that no government is justifiable only if we make a number of highly contentious assumptions about the possible range of justifications for a system of government.

With these preliminaries out of the way, let me now turn to Arrow's project.[5] An account of 'the will of the people', I suggested, would enable us, given an account of the preferences of individuals in society, to determine which social policies accord with the people's will. A social welfare function, as Arrow understands it, has a similar purpose. We begin by assuming a list of possible social states each of which represents something like a set of governmental policies (like a possible political platform). We assume further that each person in society has a preference ordering over the set of possible social states. A social welfare function, then, is a rule that assigns, to each set of individual preference orderings, a social preference ordering. We can think of this social ordering as an account of the preferences of society as a whole over the various possible sets of social policies it might adopt.

Given this minimal description of a social welfare function, it would be easy to construct any number of them. The problem becomes more interesting, however, as Arrow formulates various conditions that a social welfare function must satisfy if it is to be acceptable. To begin with, the social ordering generated by the function or rule must be expressed in terms of a relation that is *reflexive*, *complete*, and *transitive*. A relation is something like 'is preferred to' or 'is at least as good as'. The latter, but not the former, is reflexive: any object stands in this relation to itself, since any object is as good as itself. 'At least as good as' is also more general than 'preferred to' in the sense that we can define the latter in terms of the former. If we know, for each alternative, which is and which is not *at least as good as* each other, we thereby know which ones are *preferred to* which other ones. Moreover, if we define a social ordering in terms of a reflexive relation (like 'at least as good as') we can allow for the possibility of ties without sacrificing completeness. (If x and y tie, x is at least as good as y and y is at least as good as x.) To require completeness is to require that every possible social state appear on the 'list' expressing society's ordering of alternatives so that, for any pair of alternative states, the function specifies which is preferred to the other or that they are indifferent. To require transitivity, finally, is to require that the ordering defined by the social choice rule be consistent in a certain precise sense: If we call the relation in terms of which the ordering is expressed (e.g. 'at least as good as') R, then transitivity requires that, if xRy and yRz, then xRz.

Closely related to these conditions, but independent of them, is the requirement of *Unrestricted Domain*. This requires that the social welfare function assign a social ordering to *any* possible set of individual preferences. In terms of our analogy between an account of the will of the people and a social welfare function, this requirement amounts to the stipulation that the people always have a will.

In contrast to the above requirements which, I shall suggest below, derive from essentially practical concerns, Arrow imposes three other requirements on social welfare functions which seem to derive from something like ethical concerns. First, the *Pareto requirement* holds that, if for any pair of alternatives x and y everyone in society prefers x to y, then x should rank above y in the social preference ordering. Second, the *Nondictatorship* requirement holds that there must be no individual whose preferences, for each pair of alternatives, are always decisive regardless of the preferences of everyone else in society. Finally, the *Independence of irrelevant alternatives* holds that the social choice between any two alternatives must depend solely on individual preferences between those two alternatives, and must be independent of individual preferences among other alternatives or between one of the alternatives in question and some other alternative.

Given a precise, formal statement of these definitions and conditions, Arrow shows that there can be no social welfare function satisfying all of them. This conclusion, I suggested above, casts doubt on the possibility that there is a conception of the will of the people that will serve a useful purpose in democratic theory. The reason for this is that the problem of formulating a useful conception of the will of the people is in some ways analogous to the problem of devising a social welfare function. This analogy, however, requires further discussion.

2 THE RELEVANCE OF ARROW'S THEOREM

What Arrow shows is that no social welfare function, as defined, can satisfy all of the conditions he lays down. He certainly does not show that there is no possible social welfare function of *any* kind. It is clearly important, therefore, that we examine his conditions.

If we are tempted to say that a certain policy or platform represents the will of the people, we presumably mean that that policy stands in a certain relation to the preferences of individual members of society. For example, we might mean that it is preferred to some other alternative by a majority, by 60 per cent or by everyone unanimously. If we assume we will not have unanimity, the question is whether any other relation will do as an account of 'the will of the people'. Clearly not just any relation will do. A relation (something like 'preferred by a majority') will be a reasonable account of 'the will of the people' only if it satisfies certain conditions — conditions which 'preferred by the president of General Motors' presumably does not satisfy. What are these conditions? Some of the conditions Arrow lays down for a social welfare funčtion seem to be of the right sort. Thus, for example, the Nondictatorship Condition requires that social choice not be determined by the choices of just one person, regardless of the choices of others. The Pareto Condition requires that social choice be consistent with the choice of everyone when there is unanimity. Finally, the Independence of Irrelevant Alternatives requires that social choice among alternatives depend on preferences among *just* those alternatives, not, for example, on what *other* alternatives happen to be under consideration.

We can say with some plausibility, I believe, that these conditions are motivated by a desire that social choice be the choice of the people. A social welfare function satisfying these conditions would begin to look like a reasonable substitute for the notion of the will of the people. Clearly, however, some of Arrow's other conditions do not have this idea as their rationale. Among these other conditions are the requirements of transitivity, completeness, and universal domain. These conditions, I suggest, are based on considerations of something like practicality. Arrow is a welfare economist. He wants to be in a position to evaluate specific proposals or programs — to be able to say, given a proposal, whether its adoption would leave us better off than we are now. This kind of practical interest in policy evaluation helps explain the three conditions under discussion. Thus, if completeness is satisfied, we have a list of all possible social states. Given a specific policy choice we need only locate the status quo and the situation represented by the status quo plus the new proposal on the list and see which ranks higher. While completeness guarantees that every possibility will appear on the list,

Universal Domain guarantees that there will always be a list regardless of the preferences or composition of the 'electorate'.

It is important to remember at this point that Arrow's proof depends on all of the conditions he enumerates. Consequently, if we reject or alter one of these conditions it is possible that there could be a social welfare function satisfying the altered set of conditions. Given our interest in uncovering a useful conception of the will of the people, how important is the requirement of completeness? There do seem to be situations in which we would agree that a certain proposal represents the people's will, even though we are unable to say, for every pair of alternatives, which ranks higher. Consider the situation in which one proposal is preferred unanimously to any other proposal, but there is no consensus about the relation between some of the lower ranked proposals. If we define 'the will of the people' in terms of unanimity, it does seem clear in the case described what the people will. Now, if we could always define a *best* alternative, even though we lacked a complete ordering, we might be able to devise a political system that always chose this best alternative. If the best alternative were best in terms of something that could reasonably be called the people's will, we would have a system of government that constituted government by the people in an interesting sense, though our conception of the people's will did not satisfy completeness.

This will not work. We cannot have a rule that will always pick a best alternative unless completeness is satisfied![6] (Suppose completeness is not satisfied. Then there will be a pair of alternatives not ranked vis-à-vis one another. But then there will be at least one choice for which the rule specifies no best alternative.) The requirement of completeness is thus more similar to the requirement of unrestricted domain than might have been thought. The requirement that each possible alternative be ranked vis-à-vis each other possible alternative is, in effect, the requirement that, no matter how restricted the range of alternatives in a given choice situation, there will always be a choice — the people will always have a will, even if this is understood to require only specification of a best alternative or set of alternatives. This requirement is like that of unrestricted domain, then, since the latter also demands that there always be a choice, though here the idea is that there always be a choice regardless of the preference array in the society.

The point here is not that there is no such thing, ever, as the will of the people. Situations in which there is unanimity do seem to be situations in which the people have a will. But if our aim is to devise a system of government and to justify it on the ground that its laws and policies always coincide with the people's will, it looks as if we need an account of this notion according to which there always is such a thing as the people's will. Thus, the requirements of completeness and unrestricted domain do seem important. What about the third of the requirements I referred to above as 'practical', namely, transitivity?

Roughly, transitivity requires that, if x is at least as good as y, and y at least as good as z, then x must be at least as good as z. Now, if this holds, it will never happen that x is preferred to y, y to z, and z to x; and it is important that we exclude this possibility. The reason is that we are looking for a conception of the people's will to serve as a criterion for governmental policy. Yet it seems clear that we do not want a government acting on an intransitive preference ordering of the sort just described. How would it operate? Would it invest tax money to change from y to x, only to have to change to z ... and then back to y? However, while Arrow's requirement of transitivity rules out this problematic result, this requirement is stronger than it needs to be.

A condition that differs from transitivity, but still avoids the problem just mentioned, is the condition that A. K. Sen calls *acyclicity*.[7] If acyclicity holds, then, if there is an indefinite string of alternatives, the first preferred to the second, the second to the third, the third to the fourth, and so on, the first is at least as good as the last. What Sen has shown[8] is that, substituting acyclicity for transitivity, we can avoid Arrow's impossibility result. We can devise a rule or function that generates a social preference relation satisfying Arrow's conditions with acyclicity substituted for transitivity. The example that Sen offers, however, should lead us to wonder about the usefulness of his result for our purposes. The rule he states specifies that x is at least as good as y, if and only if, y is not Pareto better than x. (In general, y is Pareto better than x if and only if everyone regards y as good as x, and someone prefers y to x.) Now, for most pairs of alternatives, neither will be Pareto better than the other: someone will prefer x to y, someone else will prefer y to x. Sen achieves completeness for his rule by stipulating that, in these cases, we are to say that each is as good as the other: they are indifferent

It would be a mistake, I believe, to take this rule of Sen's to be a reasonable account of the notion of the will of the people. If we did so, we would be saying that only Pareto optimal situations accorded with the people's will, but that any such situation accorded equally with that will. (A situation is Pareto optimal if and only if there is no situation

Pareto better than it.) On this view, then, a change from one Pareto optimal situation to another would be compatible with the people's will, even though it would benefit one person at the expense of another. Similarly, a change from a suboptimal situation to *any* optimal situation would be compatible with the people's will, though — to put the point as paradoxically as possible — the choice of any particular optimal situation would be contrary to the will of those who would prefer a different optimal situation.

It is time now to sum up this discussion of Arrow's and Sen's results. I undertook the discussion because Arrow's quest for a social welfare function seemed analogous to the quest for an account of the notion of the will of the people. Hence, Arrow's impossibility theorem seemed to cast doubt on the possibility of such an account. But we have seen that at least one of Arrow's conditions — transitivity — could be modified so that we could avoid the impossibility result. And it seemed that an account of 'the will of the people' satisfying the weaker condition might still be of interest for democratic theory. On the other hand, the social choice rule suggested by Sen that satisfies the modified conditions still did not seem to be a reasonable account of the will of the people. While such an account should satisfy something close to Sen's conditions, these conditions, evidently, are not sufficient. In short, though Arrow's theorem does not force us to abandon the kind of theory of democracy we are considering in this chapter, it does provide us with an indication of how difficult it would be to save the theory.

3 AN ALTERNATIVE APPROACH

Benn and Peters, in *Principles of Political Thought*, argue against employing the notion of the will of the people in democratic theory. The will of the people, they say, 'is not a natural will'. To the extent that there is any such thing, it 'cannot be determined independently of the particular procedure [of voting] employed'.[9] 'There is no "will of the people" beyond an election result.'[10] This, of course, seems to be a blanket rejection of the approach we are considering here. However, it also suggests a rather intriguing alternative. That there is no will of the people beyond an election result does not entail that there is no will of the people at all. Quite the contrary. It suggests that the outcome of *any* election procedure (at least any procedure in which everyone participates) is *a* representation of the will of the people. So long as everyone votes, or is permitted to vote, we have popular sovereignty in as good a sense as we ever could.

This approach, which seems to turn the tables on Arrow, is intriguing, but it hardly solves our problem. What we need to do is to find a conception of the will of the people that (1) will result from some specifiable voting procedure, and (2) will justify us in believing that procedure to be desirable. The alternative suggested here ignores the problem of justification — the problem to which I shall now turn.

4 WHY POPULAR SOVEREIGNTY?

Why should we want the people to govern? Why should we think it a good thing that the people govern? It has now become evident, I hope, that the notion of the will of the people — and thus the notion of popular sovereignty — is not clear. If we are to proceed, we need to provide an account or analysis of these notions, and the discussion of Arrow's theorem has given us some idea of what we are up against if we try. The problem is to find an account of 'the will of the people' together with a description of a possible set of governmental institutions such that (1) those governmental institutions will produce legislative and policy decisions reflecting the will of the people and (2) it will clearly be desirable that government reflect the will of the people in this way. If we have all this, we will then have a theory of democracy according to which democracy, as defined, is both possible and justifiable. So far we have noted that a general justification of democracy along these lines presupposes an account of 'the will of the people' according to which the people always (or at least usually) have a will. But it also presupposes that it is *desirable* that legislation and policy reflect the people's will. Hence the questions with which I began this section.

It appears that there are at least two distinguishable reasons for thinking that the people should govern. The first has to do with the notion of moral autonomy. The concern with moral autonomy enters political theory, I think, by way of the problem of political obligation. For some,[11] the central question in evaluating the state is the question whether it legitimately exercises authority (or, as it is sometimes barbarously put, 'has legitimacy'). For those who take this line, it seems to be at least a necessary condition for a government's being a good government or a justifiable government, that it be *legitimate*, where this means that those subject to its de jure authority are also morally required to acquiesce in this authority. Now, if we say this, and also say that every person has a fundamental obligation to be autonomous — to obey only those laws or commands he issues to himself — we have a problem.[12] Under what conditions is it possible for a person to obey the state and also to discharge his obligation to be autonomous? Under what condition can a state be legitimate, where this requires that all its citizens have an obligation to obey its laws? The answer, of course, is a state in which laws and policies reflect the will of the people.

If this first line of argument is reminiscent primarily of the work of Rousseau and Kant, the second should remind us of the English liberal tradition. Briefly, the argument is this: While it is true that some acts or omissions are required by morality regardless of our wishes or desires, there are situations in which we are morally free to do whatever we wish. Governments decide questions of many different kinds, and, in the case of at least some of these questions, morality does not dictate the answer. But in these cases, where morality is silent, governmental action must respect the freedom of the citizens. In short, given the freedom of citizens, governmental action is legitimate only if it accords with the choices of the citizens. Hence, at least for a certain limited range of governmental decisions, we find ourselves again requiring popular sovereignty.

It is not *obvious* that either of these lines of argument is sound. There are premises in each argument that one might want to reject on reflection. Nevertheless, the arguments are not obviously unsound either. There is at least some reason to think that popular sovereignty is desirable. But what is the conception of popular sovereignty that is shown to be desirable by these arguments? If popular sovereignty requires that legislation accord with the will of the people, what conception of 'the will of the people' is required here? What conditions must a relevant account of 'the will of the people' satisfy? It seems to me fairly clear that the notion of the will of the people that fits these arguments requires unanimity. If we require of government that it respect the autonomy of its citizens, we cannot permit a government that requires of *any* of its citizens that he act contrary to his own will. Similarly, if we hold that people are (in some areas) free to act as they wish, then government must not coerce *anyone* to act against his wishes in these areas. In general, then, a government cannot satisfy the demands of autonomy or liberty unless its acts consistently coincide with the unanimous will of its citizens.

The trouble with the identification of the will of the people and the unanimous preference of the people is that there generally is no unanimous preference. Thus, it appears, no form of government as such is legitimate or justifiable, if it is required of a form of government that it always legislate in accordance with the unanimous will of the people. No type of government can be legitimate when there is no unanimity among citizens. The thrust of the arguments from autonomy and liberty is essentially anarchistic, not democratic. Insofar as we have an argument for the conclusion that popular sovereignty is desirable, we also have an argument to show that no government, including democratic government, is guaranteed to produce popular sovereignty.

There are two closely related responses to what I have just said. According to each, there is a kind of institutional arrangement under which real popular sovereignty, real autonomy, is possible. The first response is suggested by the work of Buchanan and Tullock[13] which will be discussed more fully in the next chapter. They make the point that even persons with different preference orderings among alternatives, given time, can usually find a program of action that is unanimously acceptable. Such a program will represent a compromise resulting from trade-offs in which each person gives in on the issues that matter less to him in turn for concessions on other issues. Hence, one might think, if we require unanimous agreement on policies and allow trade-offs, popular sovereignty can be achieved.

The second response is suggested by Robert Nozick's conception of utopia in *Anarchy, State and Utopia.*[14] Nozick describes a highly decentralized state (or world) with many distinct autonomous communities and with easy mobility from one to another. One might argue that, in such a world, each person could be completely autonomous since each could choose the community in which his or her preferences would prevail.

Each of these ideas is intriguing, and each suggests a variety of interesting topics for investigation, but neither provides a solution to the problem of authority and autonomy. Consider the first response. Though a kind of consensus, based on a compromise, is usually possible, and though it may arise if unanimity is required, a government acting on such a consensus will not therefore be a government in which each person 'gets his way'. As A. K. Sen notes, the fact that compromise is often possible 'does not . . . mean that the individual orderings must be, in general, largely unanimous'.[15] A compromise of the sort under discussion results from trade-offs. Autonomy requires that persons be able to do what they believe obligatory, but since consensus can require that one trade off some of one's moral convictions, unanimous consensus does not guarantee autonomy.

A government's operating on a rule of unanimity does not, thereby, guarantee autonomy because the need to achieve consensus or compromise among people with disparate beliefs *itself* limits individual autonomy. One is limited, in practice, by the preferences of the others with whom one associates.[16] The problem with the second proposal — the idea of decentralized government and free movement from one community to another — is similar. In government by unanimous compromise, one ends up, not with one's first choice, but with the best program one can get *consistent with the need to achieve consensus*. If there are autonomous communities, and if one chooses one's favorite as a place to live, one may still not get one's way in general. The choice of community is limited by the range of available alternatives, just as the nature of consensus is determined by the preferences of others as well as one's own. One may end up in the best of all *actual* worlds, but not thereby in the best of all *possible* worlds.

One more point concerning the utopian world of autonomous communities. Where the range of available communities is limited, or where individuals have less than perfect knowledge about the available alternatives, the possibility of easy exit from a community may actually decrease the chance of one's living in a community one really likes. Suppose no other community offers more than a slight improvement over the one I live in now, and suppose that, in fact, I could succeed in getting my way on many issues by participating in politics. If I were uncertain about my political abilities, the existence of an alternative community to which I could move might lead me to exercise the 'exit' option too quickly and end up worse off than if I had stayed put.[17]

5 SOME CONSEQUENCES

Early in this chapter I asked whether we should simply reject out of hand a theory of democracy built around the notion of popular sovereignty on the ground that it represents an unrealistic goal. I considered rejecting the ideal of rule by the people on the ground that it presupposes a unified popular will, and we almost never have that. Since then, I have looked at some attempts to give minimal sense to the notion of rule by the people, and I have asked why rule by the people might seem desirable in order to see what conditions a conception of rule by the people must satisfy if it is to play a role in a justificatory theory of democracy. The results of this investigation tend to confirm the suspicion that the notion of popular sovereignty is not particularly useful for democratic theory. There seems to be no feasible conception of democracy that will legislate only in accordance with the will of the people, and that will be justifiable for this reason.

The problem with all this is that the argument seems to be too strong. It seems not only to undermine a certain kind of justification of democracy, but also to show that no government, democratic or not, can ever be justified. The arguments from autonomy and liberty, introduced to show that popular sovereignty seemed to be at least relevant to the moral evaluation of democracy, seem to show also, if they are sound, that legitimate government is impossible. This is not the place for an extended discussion of this problem. I shall have a good deal to say about it in Chapters VI and VII. A few remarks, however, are in order here.

The argument from autonomy, I have suggested, derives from a conception of justification which, in turn, stems from a preoccupation with the problem of political obligation. There are two key assumptions in this argument: (1) a political system is justifiable only if all its citizens are morally obligated to acquiesce in its authority; and (2) no one has any moral obligations inconsistent with the fundamental obligation of autonomy. Given these two premises, it seems to follow that no government is justifiable unless it is guaranteed to govern in accordance with the unanimous will of the people. It is far from clear, however, that we ought to accept these premises. To begin with, there are certainly questions about political institutions other than the question whether citizens are obligated to obey the laws made in those institutions; and there are moral perspectives from which the answers to these questions are relevant to the evaluation of such institutions. One might ask, for example, whether institutions of a certain type are more likely than others to result in just social policies and laws. At a number of points in earlier chapters I have stressed the importance of questions about likely legislative consequences, and I have contrasted such questions with questions about procedural fairness or about whether a system encourages extensive political participation. In this chapter I have been talking about effects — about whether legislative output will correspond to an independently identified will of the people, for example — but these effects seem relevant mainly in connection with the problem of political obligation. Here, I want to reemphasize the importance of questions about the likelihood of morally good legislation, and I want to distinguish these questions from questions about political obligation. This is not to say that the two kinds of questions are altogether unrelated. It may be a necessary condition for a general obligation to obey the law that the system in which there is this obligation tend to produce just legislation. Even if this is true, however, we can give sense to the claim that a system is a good system even if it is false that people have a general obligation to obey its laws. If assumption (1) is doubtful, assumption (2) is clearly of less importance. Anyway, it is not obviously true. What does autonomy require? The idea, presumably, is that one has a fundamental obligation to act in accordance with one's own moral convictions, whatever those are. This requirement differs from a fundamental obligation to do what is in fact right. Even interpreted as statements of what one ought to do, 'all things considered', the two requirements are not logically contradictory, but neither are they equivalent. Faced with a choice between the former and the latter, why choose the former? There seem to be some rather tricky problems here. For one thing, in trying to act on the second principle, one can do no better than to act on the first. On the other hand, if we accept the second, then we must allow the possibility that someone successfully acting on the first principle may be doing the wrong thing. That is not obviously the wrong thing to say.[18]

There is a further difficulty about evaluating political institutions if we begin with the problem of political obligation, and if we also assume something like the principle of autonomy. If we start here, there will be no legitimate governments, and there will be no relevant distinctions to be drawn between different forms of government. Forms or systems of government are all equally illegitimate. If there are interesting differences between types of political institution, and if these differences affect the value of these institutions, then either the assumptions in question are false, or there is some relevant evaluative dimension other than the dimension singled out by the problem of political obligation.

So far as the argument from autonomy is concerned, then, we are not forced to conclude that no system of government is justifiable in *any* respect. Still, even if we avoid a preoccupation with the problem of political obligation and concentrate instead on the value of the likely results of a given political system, it may not be possible to avoid completely questions about the will of the people. The question here is what the morality of social policy has to do with the values and preferences of the individuals who make up society. I will explore this relationship in more detail in Chapter VI. One aspect of this question, however, does tie in with the argument from liberty that I have considered in this chapter. In many choice situations that individuals face, morality does not dictate a specific alternative, but rather leaves the choice up to the choosing parties. Since people are free to choose whatever alternative they want in these situations, I suggested, a government that legislates policy in these areas must adopt a policy that reflects the will of its citizens. Let us look again at this conclusion.

The natural thrust of the argument from liberty seems to be in the direction of limiting government, not in the direction of specifying criteria for governmental policy. If people are free to do what they want, why permit government to dictate specific actions at all? I noted this point earlier, but I also noted that, within the range of activities people are free to engage in if they wish, there are some activities that will be possible only through governmental action.[19] It was in these areas, it seemed to me, that government would be permitted to act, but would be constrained to act in accordance with the people's unanimous will. Granted that there is no guarantee of unanimity, however, what should we conclude? The conclusion suggested earlier was that no government can proceed in these areas in the absence of unanimity. However, this seems like saying that no one can have what he wants because everyone cannot have what he wants, and that seems irrational. Another possible approach is to say that, in areas in which only government coordinated activity is possible, the requirements of liberty differ from what they are in other areas. When people must coordinate their activity or not act at all, what is required – and the only thing required – is that they act on the kind of Pareto Optimal compromise solution discussed earlier.[20]

We have now come full circle. A theory of democracy based on the notion of popular sovereignty and yielding a feasible and justifiable conception of democratic government must pass a number of tests. A theory like this requires an account of what popular sovereignty involves, a sound argument to show that popular sovereignty, so conceived, is desirable or required, and an account of a kind of political system that will achieve popular sovereignty in the relevant sense. We have probed this kind of theory from a number of different angles, examining in particular the problem of formulating a reasonable conception of the will of the people and the problem of showing that the people ought to rule. Though there seemed to be some plausible arguments for the conclusion that the people should rule, we were unable to find a conception of popular sovereignty that would fit with these arguments and that was attainable. Moreover, on closer inspection, the claim that popular sovereignty is required turned out to rest on weak foundations. The ideal of popular sovereignty, though it has a certain hold on us, and though it has generated a good deal of interesting research, is, in fact, incapable of supporting a justification of democracy.

APPENDIX A: A NOTE ON THE THEORY OF REPRESENTATION

It cannot be said that there is agreement among theorists about when a government is representative or about when one individual represents another. An account with a certain plausibility, however, states that one person represents another when the former acts for the latter, where 'acting for' is understood as 'acting in the interest of'.[21] A representative government is a government in which citizens' representatives make political decisions. This account of representation and representative government gives rise to several kinds of questions. First, when is it true that one person represents another in this sense? Must my representative act on my opinion of my interests, or on his own opinion? When is it true that an individual represents a constituency, where the constituency may consist of persons with diverse interests?[22] Second, how do we achieve representative government? What kind of political institutions do we need if we are to ensure that those making decisions in government actually do represent citizens?[23] Third, why should we want representative government as characterized here?

Parts of my argument in this chapter are relevant to the first and third kinds of question mentioned here. Thus, for example, we might argue that representing people's interests involves respecting their preferences — acting on their will; and we might go on to argue that government by representatives of the people will tend to reflect the will of the people. Thus, representative government might be recommended as the best institutionalization of the ideal of popular sovereignty. If this is the argument for representative government, however, it is doubly flawed. It presupposes a conception of the will of the people at two levels: it assumes that each constituency has a specifiable will, and it assumes that the nation as a whole has a will in some morally interesting sense. The first assumption seems dubious, and the second even more so. This is not, of course, the only kind of argument for what we

69

normally think of as representative institutions. While it does raise some questions about the concept of representation of a constituency, it leaves open the possibility that the kind of accountability we find in a system in which people elect representatives is desirably on other grounds.

APPENDIX B:
MAJORITY RULE, TRANSITIVITY AND UNANIMITY

Arrow's problem, on my interpretation, is to offer an analysis of 'the will of the people'. His immediate aim is not to lay down criteria for evaluating voting rules, nor is it to examine voting rules in the light of such criteria. Still, certain of his results seem to raise questions about the acceptability of voting procedures like majority rule. In particular, the method of majority rule can result in intransitivities: x defeats y, y defeats z and z defeats x. Earlier, I went along with the idea that an account of 'the will of the people' should not result in an intransitive social preference ordering, and so, it would seem, I should not endorse a voting procedure that might lead to intransitivities.

Under certain clearly defined circumstances, it has been noted, the method of majority voting cannot yield intransitivities: It cannot yield intransitivities if the preference orderings of the members of the electorate are all 'single peaked'.[24] However, I have also endorsed the requirement of universal domain, requiring that 'the will of the people' be defined for any possible set of preference orderings in society. To require that preferences be single peaked would be to reject this other requirement. (By analogy, I rejected an account of 'the will of the people' as their *unanimous* will on the ground that it left the notion undefined for most cases.) Just as I reject accounts of 'the will of the people' which leave it undefined in many cases, should I not also reject a voting procedure that will lead to problems, like intransitivities, in some possible cases?

I believe there is an important difference between justifying a voting procedure and justifying an account of 'the will of the people' where the latter is to be used in the kind of justification of democracy discussed in this chapter. In Chapter VI, I shall argue in favor of a system of government operating on majority rule, and I shall argue that, over at least those issues involving matters of moral importance, various features of the system other than the voting rule will tend to create a consensus on those matters. Hence, intransitivities will not often arise. The idea here is that the political system will affect the preferences of citizens in such a way that the pattern of preferences will not have certain problematic features. But it is important to see that this kind of option is not open to someone who wants to define 'the will of the people' and defend some system of government on the ground that it tends to reflect that will. If this kind of theory has any justificatory force at all, it would seem, it must take the preferences of people as given. We do not have an independent justification for a political system in the fact that it reflects the will of the people if that system *also* works to affect what that will is.

There is a second point here. Suppose that, in a system operating on majority rule, there are some situations in which voting on every pair of alternatives would result in an intransitive ordering. In most actual voting procedures this fact will never show up, but the result of voting will simply be determined by the order in which alternatives are introduced.[25] In practice, societies will not find themselves shifting from z to y, to x, back to z . . . and so on. I believe that this possibility does not constitute an overwhelming general objection to a voting procedure. But, *if* we argue for a voting rule on the ground that it reflects the will of the people, and then adopt a conception of this latter notion according to which the people's will is represented by an intransitive ordering, we do have a problem. If the social decision procedure is supposed actually to reflect the independently defined popular will, and if this will is intransitive, then it would seem that social decisions must actually reflect this intransitivity. It must somehow enact all (or none?) of the cyclicly ranked alternatives. But, again, this problem becomes acute only in the context of a theory that insists on popular sovereignty as here defined.

V

ECONOMIC THEORIES

Economists typically proceed by constructing abstract models of the interactions of economic entities against the background of specified economic institutions: utility maximizing individuals choose among the products of competing, profit maximizing firms, each equipped with fixed and variable costs. Individuals with fixed incomes invest fixed amounts of money in various bundles of goods and services, and so on. The structure of these models is essentially deductive. Given a characterization of several highly abstract entities operating in the economy, it is possible to derive a surprising number of interesting conclusions about their behavior in certain circumstances and about their reciprocal effects on one another. It is thus possible to show how individual utility functions combined with price ratios, for example, affect the composition of the bundles of goods individuals select and how these selections affect further things like the allocation of resources among different possible uses.

When economists turn to the analysis of democracy, they proceed in much the same way. Among the main actors we again find utility maximizing individuals, but they now deal in votes instead of money; political parties seeking to govern now take the place of firms seeking to maximize profits; and governmental policies benefitting the voters now take the place of goods and services produced by firms. At least, these changes may take place, but whether they do will depend on the precise nature of the democratic system being subjected to analysis. This last point, of course, is quite general. Economists can construct analytical models of different kinds of political system, and they can also construct analytical models of different kinds of economic system. For example, in the case of democratic political systems, it is possible to construct a model of a direct democracy in which decisions result from the votes of citizens or of indirect democracy in which, to recall Schumpeter's adumbration of economic theories, a political party makes basic governmental decisions after winning a competitive struggle for the votes of the people. Similarly, whichever of these systems we choose to study, we can vary the subject by varying such things as voting rules or such background constitutional constraints as the prohibition of vote buying or trading.

Economic theories of democracy will differ from one another, then, according as they are theories of different kinds of democratic polity. Nevertheless, what I shall call economic theories here do have certain things in common: their abstract deductive character, their assumption of rational utility maximization on the part of individuals, and their tendency to regard the political process on analogy with the market as a mechanism that amalgamates individual preferences, exogenously determined, so as to determine a set of government policy decisions. What determines governmental policy decisions is the interaction of individual preferences and a specific set of political institutions. The interest of the theory lies in its presumed ability to predict the legislative effects of changes in political institutions ('the rules of the political game') or of changes in the pattern of preferences prevailing in society. (The ability of the theory to predict accurately depends, of course, on whether its models, admittedly abstracted from reality, nevertheless retain the salient features of reality.)[1]

An economic theory of democracy as described so far is clearly not a full theory of the sort that this book is about. Economic theories, as described so far, do not attempt to say what democracy is, to establish its possibility and then to justify or otherwise evaluate it. Instead, they are designed to describe or predict how democratic systems operate. Still, they do embody an account of what democracy is in the sense that they presuppose such an account. The systems the economic theorists study are more or less idealized, abstract versions of contemporary institutions in western countries. Hence, we can say that democracy, as it is understood by the economic theorists, is roughly what we have in America. Moreover, except insofar as the systems studied are *idealizations* of present reality, it is clear that there is little problem about establishing the possibility of democracy as defined. Whether the economic theorists mean to be evaluating democratic institutions, as opposed to just describing them, is a rather more difficult question. The theorists

I will discuss here differ from one another in this respect. In any case, it seems to me clear that an understanding of how a type of political system operates is a prerequisite for intelligent evaluation of that type of system. Given the account we find in economic theories, moreover, certain justifications (and criticisms) suggest themselves. If the economic theorists do not mean to be offering what I think of as a full theory of democracy, then, it is still possible to construct an interesting theory of this type built on their work. That is what I shall be doing in this chapter.

1 AN EXAMPLE OF ECONOMIC ANALYSIS: THE INTENSITY PROBLEM

One of the problems that concerns theorists interested in the justification of majoritarian democracy is the so called 'intensity problem'. There seems to be a reasonably clear sense in which a system of majority rule gives each citizen equal political power,[2] yet this kind of equal power and citizen sovereignty seems to be compatible with legislative outcomes detrimental to the interests of substantial portions of the citizenry: for every majority that approves of a certain proposal, there is a minority that does not. This fact in itself does not show that the system treats people unequally or is objectionable in any other respect, but there might be a problem if we note that the majority may be an 'apathetic majority' and the minority an 'intense minority'. If 51 per cent of the electorate has a slight preference for A over B, and votes that preference, while 49 per cent have a strong preference for B over A it begins to appear that the kind of equality embodied in majority rule may be the wrong kind of equality. Equal political power for *persons* does not guarantee a regard for preferences proportional to their strength. We seem to be faced with one version of the problem of the tyranny of the majority.[3]

There are serious questions, some of which I shall examine at the end of this chapter, about the relevance of the intensity problem to the moral evaluation of majoritarian democracy. Quite apart from these questions, however, is the question whether (or how often) apathetic majorities will actually be able to enact policies over intense minority opposition. What kind of policies will a government adopt in a representative democracy operating under majority rule? This is one of the kinds of question economic theories attempt to answer. Consider the following simplified model derived from Anthony Downs's *An Economic Theory of Democracy*.[4] Suppose that:

1 The central administration makes governmental decisions on each type of policy;
2 There are only two alternative course of action in each policy area;
3 The choice in each policy area is independent of the choice in any other area;
4 There are two parties, one of which is the incumbent administration;
5 Each part knows which voters prefer which alternative for each choice and by how much they prefer the preferred alternative;
6 Voters are fully informed and vote so as to maximize utility.

Under these conditions, Downs reasons, the incumbent has no alternative but to institute the alternative, in each policy area, supported by the larger number of voters. (Suppose the incumbents supported a minority position on one or more issues. If so, the opposition party could win the next election simply by matching the incumbent's platform on every issue except one of those on which the incumbent went with the minority. On that issue alone, the opposition would win.)[5]

Under these simplified conditions, it appears that no minority on any issue will ever get its way. The best strategy for an opposition party seems to be the strategy of adopting the incumbent's platform and hoping that voters will put more faith in the opposition's ability to carry out its program efficiently. It turns out, however, that there are exceptions to this generalization, the most interesting of which involves a coalition of minorities. It is best illustrated by an example. Suppose there are two policy areas, A and B, and there are two alternatives in each area, A, A' and B, B'. Suppose further that there are eleven voters, and that A would defeat A' six to five, and B would defeat B' six to five. An incumbent party following the majority strategy would adopt a platform favoring A and B. But now suppose that, of the six favoring A, five favor B', and feel more strongly about the latter preference than about the former. Similarly, of the six favoring B, five favor A', and feel more strongly about the latter preference. In general, then, when we look at preference orderings for *platforms*, five voters have the ordering represented by column I, and five others have the ordering represented by column II. (Alternatives higher on the list are preferred to those lower.)

I	II
AB'	A'B
A'B'	A'B'
A B	A B
A' B	A B'

Though the incumbent party, following the majority strategy, enacts A B, instead of A' B', the latter combination is preferred to the former by ten voters out of eleven. Under these conditions, the opposition party can defeat the incumbents by adopting the platform A' B' and winning the support of a coalition of intense minorities.[6]

What of Downs's claim that, under the special conditions 1-6 above, an incumbent should adopt the majority strategy? The coalition of minorities case does not show this to be false. It just shows that the majority strategy is no *guarantee* for the incumbent party. Moreover, we should note that the tenure in office of the opposition party (which does not follow the majority strategy) will be short. They support A' B', but the five voters represented by Table 1 prefer A B' to this; and the five in Table II prefer A' B. One of these two combinations can now defeat the (one time) opposition. Which one wins will depend on the preferences of the eleventh voter. The situation is not stable.

The conclusions here are derived entirely from general assumptions — assumptions about the voting rule, the number of parties, the motivation of the parties and voters, and the like. Thus, we have an example of the kind of approach typical of economic analyses of democracy. The conclusion that a coalition of intense minorities can sometimes defeat a majority government is an interesting conclusion from the perspective of someone interested in the problem of intensity as described by Dahl.[7] Even more interesting, however, is the suggestion implicit in this example of a close analogy between the operation of a democratic political system and a market economy. The way in which intensities of preference enter into the formation of a coalition of minorities is analogous to the way in which intensities of preference affect economic transactions in the marketplace. The minorities in the example do not openly engage in vote trading, but they could have. If so, their agreement to vote for A' B' would have been like a business deal in which both parties to the transaction give up something, but each is better off than he would have been without the transaction. Each would give up what he cares less about in order to get what he cares more about. When we apply the techniques of economic analysis to the study of democratic politics, then, one of the interesting results is that democratic politics seem to work in a way similar to the way in which the market works.

It is widely conceded that the free market economy, under certain optimal conditions, tends to have desirable social consequences. It is clearly interesting to inquire, then, to what extent a democratic political system is like the market. Alternatively, it is interesting to examine the possibility of constructing a political system more nearly analogous to a market economy than is the present system. Specifically, since one great advantage of free exchange in the market is that it is supposed to lead to an optimal allocation of goods, can we structure a political system that will similarly achieve optimal allocations of benefits to citizens? The writers who have done most to develop this line of thought are James Buchanan and Gordon Tullock in *The Calculus of Consent.*[8]

Why does the market lead to optimal outcomes? Roughly, and in the simplest kind of case, people trade what they care less about for what they care more about; and they continue to trade until there are no mutually beneficial trades left to make. Consider the classic trading diagram[9] for a two person case:

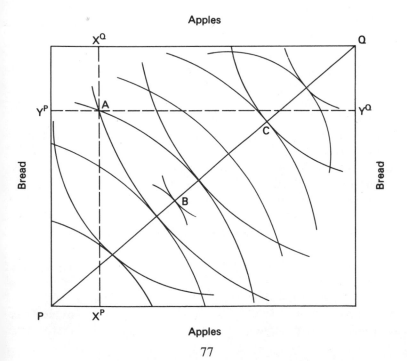

The rectangle represents the total quantity of apples and bread in the possession of two person, P and Q. Any particular point within the rectangle, A for example, represents a certain distribution of these goods between P and Q. At A, P has x^p apples and y^p loaves of bread, while Q has x^q apples and y^q loaves of bread. The curves emanating from and convex to the southwest and northeast corners are indifference curves for, respectively, P and Q. P would like a distribution of goods represented by a point lying on one of his indifference curves as far to the northeast as possible. Q prefers distributions as far to the southwest as possible. For most initial distributions of goods, it will be possible for both parties to improve their situations by trading. There are exceptions, however. Consider the point C. Point C is a point at which one of Q's indifference curves is tangent to one of P's curves. Any movement from point C – any redistribution of goods – must move either P or Q to a lower indifference curve. There is no mutually beneficial redistribution, and so, if each is rational, there will be no trading. Now consider point A. Relative to point A, there is at least one point – e.g. point B – representing an improvement for both P and Q. Thus, if point A represents the initial distribution, P and Q will have an incentive to trade. P would be willing to give up some bread for more apples, and Q would be willing to give up some apples for more bread. Any distribution within the area enclosed by the two curves that intersect at A represents an improvement for both, relative to A. Only when the traders have arrived at a distribution like that at point B – a distribution represented by a point of tangency between two indifference curves – will the trading cease. The curve determined by the set of such points of tangency is called, for obvious reasons, the contract curve. The points on this curve are also, by definition, Pareto optimal points. At any such point, there is no way for one person to be better off without the other being worse off. If we start with a distribution like that at A, and if the traders are rational, any trade will leave them within the area enclosed by the two curves intersecting at A, and the result will represent a Pareto *improvement* relative to A: at least one person will be better off, and neither will be worse off. When trading ceases, on the contract curve, they will be at a Pareto *optimum* that is a Pareto *improvement* on the initial distribution. (The precise point they reach will depend on luck, clever bargaining, etc. But, if they are rational, it will be somewhere between the two curves intersecting at the point of initial distribution.)

This account of trading, and of how trading will work out, depends on a number of assumptions. It assumes, as already noted, that traders will act rationally in the sense that each will act voluntarily only in ways which move him to a higher indifference curve (or, at least, do not move him to a lower one). Moreover, the claim that traders will eventually end up on the contract curve assumes that bundles of goods are divisible; it assumes that each person will be able to vary the ratio of goods he holds (of apples to bread) until the distribution between the two puts them precisely on the contract curve. (If, for some reason, the two could trade only in units of crates of bread and bushels of apples, they might be frustrated in their attempt to reach the contract curve.) Finally, it assumes that no redistribution takes place except by mutual consent — by unanimous agreement. (Thus, it assumes enforcement of property rules.) It is this assumption, together with the assumption of rationality, that guarantees redistributions that are Pareto improvements. These assumptions also guarantee that the final outcome will be determined in part by the initial distribution. If the initial distribution is very unequal, the outcome after trading will also be unequal, even though it results from mutual agreement.

With this discussion of economic exchange behind us, let us return to the intensity problem. The problem, recall, is that the operation of majority rule might lead to changes in governmental policy desired (weakly) by a bare majority but intensely disliked by a large minority. A change like this in governmental policy is very different from the kind of change that normally results from economic exchange, since changes of the latter kind are typically Pareto improvements (at least for those taking part in the exchange). How could we modify the political system to make its operation more like the operation of the market? One obvious change is to shift from majority rule to a unanimity rule, for, as we saw in the general analysis of trade, it is partly because economic exchange requires mutual consent that it results in Pareto improvements. But how is a unanimity rule to work, since a presupposition of the intensity problem is that there is disagreement between the majority and the minority? It is Buchanan and Tullock who propose that we reconsider the unanimity rule, and they say theorists have been too quick to reject it because they have paid too much attention to the lack of unanimity on individual issues taken one at a time (ch. 7). The intense minority and apathetic majority may not agree on the specific issue in question, but the minority might persuade the majority to vote the minority position on this issue in exchange for some concession on another issue about which some members of the majority feel more strongly. In short, if we require unanimity, but permit vote trading, or logrolling, the political process will indeed look a lot like the market, and it appears that the political process will result in decisions which, taken together, will leave everyone better off. (One of the interesting things about the economic analysis of democracy is that it suggests an argument in favor of practices, like logrolling, that are widely condemned by other theories.) Under this kind of system, there will be no suffering intense minorities — or, if some suffer on some issue, we can be assured that they will be compensated on other issues. In general, we can expect the political process to eventuate in something close to Pareto optimal outcomes, though attainment of an optimum will depend in part on the divisibility of 'goods', i.e., of policies.

2 BUCHANAN AND TULLOCK'S RATIONALE FOR DEMOCRACY

Downs's primary aim is to use the techniques of economic analysis to develop a descriptive model of the operation of a democratic system of government. Given such a model, he notes,[10] the normative theorist will be in a position to assess democracy in terms of his moral principles; but Downs himself does not enter into the fray. Buchanan and Tullock, on the other hand, are interested in questions of justification at least to the extent that they want to inquire into the kind of normative perspective that would lead a theorist to prefer democracy.[11] It is this interest which leads them to explore constitutional arrangements that are alternatives to established systems. Their techniques of analysis, however, are typical economic techniques like those of Downs.

My discussion, above, of the advantages of the market and of the way in which a political system requiring unanimity would work already contains a good deal of Buchanan and Tullock's argument for a political system embodying market features. I shall turn now to a more systematic presentation of their views. They choose to appraise systems of government from a kind of contractarian point of view — from the perspective of a constitutional convention. They assume a group of rational, utility maximizing citizens, and they ask what kind of political system such citizens would agree to unanimously. Each, it is assumed, will choose a government in which he has the best chance of attaining his own ends while protecting those gains he is able to make independent of government (ch. 2). At this point, however, things become more complicated. On the one hand, Buchanan and Tullock regard the first question facing the citizens as the question of the proper realm of governmental action. Independent of questions about optimal voting rules are questions about the kind of decisions that will be made with such rules. At the same time, however, they choose to ' "jump over" the minimal collectivization of activity that is involved in the initial definition of human and property rights and the enforcement of sanctions against violations of these rights' (46). So, while state activity is to some extent in need of justification from the perspective of the original contract situation, all such activity does not need this kind of justification.

Assuming a basic specification of rights, then, there remains the question what else the government should be authorized to do. From the economist's perspective, the natural answer is *nothing*. After all, the standard analysis of free market exchange tells us that, given enforcement of basic property rights, together with enforcement of contracts and the like, each can expect to gain from the unfettered operation of the market. This assumes, however, that there are no *external* costs or benefits. It assumes that, when A is in a position to benefit B, A will be encouraged to do so because he will be able to require payment from B; and it assumes that A will be discouraged from gaining benefits at the expense of others — imposing costs on them — because they will be able to demand payment in compensation.

In the simple trading model, we thought in terms of just two kinds of benefit (gains in apples or bread) and two kinds of cost (loss of apples or bread). Supposing enforcement of laws against force and fraud, each person can withhold benefits from the other pending payment, and neither can impose costs on the other without making payment. External costs are those for which one cannot, effectively, demand compensation and external benefits are those for which one cannot, effectively, be required to pay. Which costs or benefits are external depends in part on property institutions, but it is clear that in most societies there are externalities. Air and water pollution are classic examples of external costs, and it is widely held that public education and national defense involve external benefits.

When there are possible external costs or benefits, the operation of the market does not guarantee that all changes will be Pareto improvements, and it does not guarantee that all Pareto improvements will be made. It is possible that some uncompensated harms can be prevented only by coercive governmental action, and it is possible that some benefits will be produced only with governmental incentives. The price

81

system will not provide the normal incentives. Because of the problem of externalities, Buchanan and Tullock argue that a government more extensive than the government enforcing basic personal and property rights may seem desirable from the perspective of those designing the constitution. Roughly, they would want a kind of limited government that would intervene in the market in those areas that involve significant externalities. More precisely, they would want coercive interference in those areas in which they could reasonably expect the benefits of interference to exceed the possible costs (ch. 5).

It is a fundamental assumption of Buchanan and Tullock's analysis that government, while it can act to limit costs or produce benefits, is also likely to *impose* costs on individuals with no compensating benefits. It does so, for example, whenever it raises general taxes to support a program that benefits only a portion of the population. Given specified voting rules, constitutional designers would want to limit the range of government activity to those areas in which the government, operating under the specified rules, would tend to produce greater benefits than costs for each. Alternatively, instead of trying to anticipate the areas in which government might impose net costs on individuals, they could adopt voting rules that would automatically preclude imposition of net external costs. It is this second approach that Buchanan and Tullock find most intriguing. From the perspective of the constitutional convention, they argue, the best system for making social decisions is a system operating by a unanimity rule with an open market in votes. Majority rule is not the natural first solution to the problem of social decision-making; it is at best a sort of compromise to which people are driven because of the time consuming 'transaction costs' involved in reaching unanimity. Ideally, then, ignoring transaction costs, rational persons at the constitutional convention would permit governmental intervention (either to prevent costs or produce benefits) only when intervention in a particular case is unanimously acceptable or is part of a program that is unanimously acceptable.

The idea here, clearly, is to preserve the attractive features of the market in the political system. Noting that the market may fail to achieve Pareto optimal results without coercive intervention, Buchanan and Tullock reluctantly admit that some such intervention may be necessary. However, they then opt for the same principle of mutual agreement that governs market transactions as the fundamental rule for political decision-making. Given this rule, the operation of the market, together with the operation of the political system, should lead society to a Pareto optimal situation via a series of Pareto improvements. A system that will do that would be unanimously acceptable from the perspective of the constitutional convention. Each will expect to improve his situation in the long run. This, I take it, is Buchanan and Tullock's ideal, together with their argument for it. They go on to argue, however, that something closer to majority rule might be preferable all things considered, given the costs of reaching consensus (ch. 8). Given vote trading, they argue, majority rule would lead to Pareto optimality, but not necessarily via Pareto improvements (ch. 12). They interpret the kind of checks and balances in the United States' system — the bicameral legislature, for example — as attempts to limit the operation of the simple majority rule, pulling us back toward the requirement of unanimity and thus limiting the possibility of external costs imposed by government (ch. 16).

This completes my rather compressed account of Buchanan and Tullock's theory. Is it a reasonable theory? How convincing is the argument for unanimity? for majority rule? In what follows, I shall appraise this theory from two distinguishable, but not entirely distinct, perspectives. I shall examine it first from an internal point of view, considering whether utility maximizing individuals in Buchanan and Tullock's constitutional convention really would favor the kind of system they advocate. Next, I shall turn to external criticism, questioning the perspective of the constitutional convention as the right normative perspective, and raising some rather difficult questions about the particular brand of individualism that seems to underlie Buchanan and Tullock's theory.

3 INTERNAL CRITICISM

In Chapter II, I discussed briefly some of the formal properties of voting rules, and I noted a difference between simple majority rule and special majority or unanimity rules: the latter fail to satisfy a condition of *neutrality*, since they embody a bias in favor of the status quo. If we are interested in the intrinsic fairness of voting rules, and if neutrality is essential to fairness, we should reject a unanimity rule. But Buchanan and Tullock are concerned with an apparently different question, namely, would rational utility maximizers in a constitutional convention choose this rule?

The persons in the constitutional convention are not in a state of nature. As noted earlier, they are choosing within a minimal state that has given an initial definition of property rights and human rights and that protects those rights. It is against the background of these institutions that they must choose a system for making social decisions that will govern any subsequent changes. Each must ask himself, given the initial status quo, what kind of changes he would like to see made, what kind of changes others are likely to want, and, given answers to these questions, how easy it should be to make changes. Intuitively, those who are dissatisfied with the initial property distribution would want a rule that would make changes easier, while those who are satisfied would want a conservative rule. More specifically, those who are dissatisfied would not want the range of possible changes restricted to Pareto improvements since such improvements, though they tend to leave each better off, still preserve over-all inequalities. (If the initial distribution in a trading situation is unequal, the result of trade will be similarly unequal.) Those who are satisfied with their initial endowment of goods, on the other hand, would like a voting rule that made change difficult. It is not just obvious then, that there would be unanimous agreement on the conservative rule of unanimity, even if we disregard transaction costs.

This line of criticism is a natural one, but it must be developed carefully. It seems to be based on the idea that the initial definition and enforcement of property rules establishes a fixed, unchangeable distribution of wealth, and that those who are initially disadvantaged will be unable to improve their lot except through the action of government. But this is a mistake. A system of property rules and personal rights, as Buchanan and Tullock surely understand it, does not ossify a particular pattern of distribution. Rather, it constitutes a kind of framework within which, at the very least, the kind of market exchange discussed above can take place. But now it is important to note that this kind of market exchange represents only a very small part of economic activity. Trading takes place only when there is mutual agreement, and so it does not result in fundamental changes in distributive patterns. Other kinds of economic exchange, however, can result in fundamental changes: lucky investments taking advantage of disequilibrium in capital markets can create new fortunes overnight; similarly, technological innovation in a certain industry, exhaustion of old natural resources, discovery of new uses for others, and the like, can all lead to such changes. Consequently, it would be a mistake to assume that someone badly off at the time of the constitutional convention could expect no improvement in his situation except through the actions of government. Even a poor person might feel that he had more to fear from an active, interventionist government than from a laissez faire state because he might calculate that he had a good chance to do well on his own. The dynamic nature of laissez faire society seems to mitigate the force of one kind of objection to Buchanan and Tullock's theory: it is not obvious that the poor would want a system in which political change was easy to come by. But, for the same reason, it is not obvious that those who are well off at the time of the convention would want a system in which change is hard to come by. There are various ways to lose one's fortune without the help of government (though there may be even more ways to safeguard it). More interesting though, in the context of Buchanan and Tullock's theory, is the problem of externalities. The reason for having a government – over and above the minimal one – is that it is supposed to reduce external costs and produce external benefits. But just how is it supposed to reduce external costs? Presumably, there is a problem because the initial property laws do not already rule out all possible actions that would impose costs on others. Thus, they permit changes that are not Pareto improvements. If a petrochemical firm makes use of the air or water in such a way as to damage my lungs or my property, the price system does not provide me with any way to charge the firm for the use of these resources. Very likely, indeed, I do not even have a way to exact compensation through the courts. The government's function in Buchanan and Tullock's system is to correct this situation – to get the firm to stop polluting or to compensate me for the damage that I have suffered. But how is the government supposed to do that if we require unanimity? Why will the owners of the firm agree to the limitations?

Buchanan and Tullock argue that, in principle, it is possible to solve this kind of problem by mutual consent even without government. Those who are damaged by the pollution – if they really *are* being damaged – can get together to buy off the polluter (90-1).[12] And this is just what will happen in a government operating on the unanimity rule. There will be unanimous agreement on some proposal providing relief for those who suffered damage and providing compensation for the polluter in turn. For example, those who suffered damage might agree to have their taxes raised on condition that the government provide a subsidy to the firm to pay for the installation of antipollution equipment. But now note what has happened. Relative to the situation that obtained after pollution started, everyone is better off because of governmental action — otherwise there would have been no unanimous agreement. Relative to the situation before the firm started polluting, however, the owners of the firm are better off, but its victims are worse off. The operation of the free market together with a government operating on the unanimity rule has led to a change that is not a Pareto improvement. Moreover, the change is, intuitively, the wrong one: if anyone should be worse off than before the pollution began, it is the owners of the firm. The important point, however, is this: so long as there is potential for externalities in the private sector, the existence of a government operating on the rule of unanimity does not guarantee that all future changes will have the net effect of a Pareto improvement.

Buchanan and Tullock present the idea of a government requiring unanimous consent for its actions as a reasonable solution to the problem of constitutional choice on the ground that it provides a kind of security. It allows people to make those changes that can be expected to bring mutual benefits, but it prevents governmental action that will benefit some at the expense of others. I have argued, however, that the case for this rule is not as straightforward as it may seem. Those who have little at the time of the constitutional convention may be less interested in security — protection of what they have — than those who have a lot to lose from redistributionist policies. The dynamic nature of the free market, private sector of the economy, however, makes it difficult to argue unequivocally that the poor would prefer a government operating on a less restrictive rule; but the potential for external diseconomies in the market also makes it less obvious that those interested solely in protecting what they have would want such a restrictive rule.

Two more points should be noted. First, a rather minor point: it is clear that Buchanan and Tullock are concerned about the potential for mischief at the hands of government. This concern is not unreasonable. But it is worth noting that, for the same reason that the unanimity rule makes it difficult to change the status quo by governmental action, it also makes it difficult to alter governmental policies adopted in the past. Yet it seems likely that some such policies will be seen, once adopted, to be mistakes. Second, when we think of the process of reaching consensus — especially when we think in terms of economic exchange in the market — we naturally assume (statistically) normal desires and interests. In the example discussed earlier, we assume that people want to increase their holdings of bread and apples, and that that is their main motivation. But Buchanan and Tullock, from the beginning, place no restrictions on the range of possible utility functions. Suppose the traders differed in race, and one refused to deal with any member of the other's race. In that case, they would make no trades because, in terms of their full scales of preference, they would already be at a Pareto optimum; even if one would benefit from trade, the other would not, since the act of trading itself would be overwhelmingly repugnant to him. This history of racism, it seems to me, testifies to the fact that examples like this are not altogether fanciful. I shall have more to say about the problem of extreme utility functions in the next section. Here, I simply want to point out that it is a further factor which obviously must complicate the calculations of those participating in the constitutional convention.

4 EXTERNAL CRITICISM

So far, I have questioned whether Buchanan and Tullock's ideal form of government is most desirable even from their own preferred normative perspective. I now want to broaden the discussion, considering both further kinds of argument in favor of their system and also further criticisms.

I suggested earlier that the appeal of the requirement of unanimous consent lies in its providing a kind of security against government encroachments into the lives of individuals. A stronger argument might be that this system protects individual moral rights. The kind of governmental action on which Buchanan and Tullock concentrate takes place against a background of protected personal and property rights. If we suppose that all moral rights are protected by the system of basic protections, and if we also suppose that all moral rights are legitimately alienable, it would then *appear* that a system protecting those rights but permitting further governmental action when there is unanimous consent would be a justifiable system from the perspective of a theory of natural rights. (The assumption that basic property laws and laws protecting personal rights protect *moral* rights would be a useful assumption for Buchanan and Tullock because it would validate their decision to 'jump over' the initial stage of political collectivization without justification. But they make no such assumption explicitly.)

There are two kinds of objection to this justification. The first objection is connected with the dynamic features of the basic system of rights discussed earlier. If our theory of moral rights requires maintenance of some specific pattern of distribution, the kind of system of property rights envisioned by Buchanan and Tullock will not suffice to ensure a morally acceptable system. But even if our theory of moral rights permits alterations in the pattern of distribution, so long as these occur in legitimate ways,[13] it is not clear that any specific system of legal rules will serve to protect moral rights indefinitely through exogenous changes like changes in technology. The problem I have in mind is analogous to the problem of externalities in the private sector that I discussed earlier. Any system of property or personal rights will provide protection against various kinds of encroachment by others. As social conditions change, however, new kinds of encroachment are discovered, e.g., pollution. Whether these kinds of encroachment constitute violations of moral rights will be a matter for moral decision. Some surely will, however, and a system that prevents change in the laws in the absence of unanimous consent may well not be responsive enough to continue to protect moral rights.

The second objection concerns the progress of generations. Even supposing that the laws protecting basic personal and property rights protect all such moral rights, Buchanan and Tullock's system will protect moral rights only if these are legitimately alienable. Otherwise even unanimously acceptable changes might violate rights. But what one generation gives up willingly subsequent generations might not be willing to give up; and when changes require unanimity, it is difficult to return to the situation prior to the alienation of rights.

It should be emphasized that Buchanan and Tullock do not try to defend their conception of democracy in terms of the kind of natural rights position I have discussed here, and so my objections to this position do not apply directly to their theory. Nevertheless, it is interesting that a defense of their theory couched in terms of moral rights runs afoul of objections very much like objections that apply to their contractarian argument, namely, the objection concerning externalities in the private sector and the objection concerning the difficulty of correcting for past mistakes under the unanimity rule. Still, it is possible to argue that these objections are relatively minor. Granted, the political system Buchanan and Tullock envision will fail to prevent some uncompensated costs, and may fail to provide some collective benefits, but perhaps it will do as well in these respects as any other possible system. They are well aware of the need to compromise with reality in some matters as is evidenced by their consideration of transaction costs and consequent willingness to shift from the unanimity rule to majority rule.

(If my objections to the unanimity rule are sound, this shift may be more advantageous than they contemplate.) True, they continue to argue that under majority rule, given full side payments, the system will achieve Pareto optimal outcomes and that, consequently, 'in an expectational sense' (176) it is optimal from the perspective of each person at the constitutional convention. So, it is worth noting Downs's persuasive argument to the effect that, in the real world, attainment of Pareto optimality in a system of majority rule is unlikely given technical problems of indivisibility, lack of rationality, lack of knowledge, problems about the pricing of votes where there is vote buying, and so forth.[14] But the question remains whether this is merely nit-picking. After all, the market does not always achieve Pareto optimal outcomes either, but it comes reasonably close and probably does better than any alternative.

The real question about the economic theory of democracy is not whether the justification it employs is successful in every detail but whether that kind of justification is appropriate for a political system. Buchanan and Tullock's appeal to a constitutional convention of rational utility maximizers is reminiscent of Singer's argument for the fairness of democratic procedures (Chapter II, Section 2, above). I criticized this kind of justification on the ground that it ignored the importance of the likely outcomes of the system to its justification. Here Buchanan and Tullock seem to be on firmer ground since they imagine the participants at the convention assessing constitutions in terms of their outcomes. Thus they focus on the way in which the democratic political system takes account of and satisfies the desires of citizens. The argument is like the argument for the market economy in terms of 'consumer sovereignty': the system is flexible, adapting to the desires of citizens, and its tendency to Pareto optimality means that it satisfies desires efficiently without waste. (If it is possible to make some better off without making anyone worse off, then a system that tends towards optimality will do so.) The emphasis is not on the kind of equal *chance* of influencing policy that is compatible with *no one's* having any influence in the end. Instead the emphasis is on satisfying desires as fully as possible, given technological limitations and, of course, conflicts among the desires seeking satisfaction. In sum, the argument seems — or can be made to seem — far more like a utilitarian argument than like an argument based on a notion of fair procedures.

In spite of these differences of emphasis, however, the economic argument is also in some respects importantly like the fairness argument.

While emphasis is on satisfaction of desire, the system of majority rule, at least, is neutral among desires and preferences. While participants in the constitutional convention choose among constitutions in terms of their likely consequences, they are not assumed to share an interest in any specific kind of consequence. Their one assumed common bond is that they are utility maximizers: they have preferences and they want these preferences met. The neutrality of the system among preferences is simply a reflection of its unanimous acceptability to future citizens with unspecified desires. The economic conception of democracy, and its corresponding argument for democracy, is not based on indifference to outcomes; but its conception of a desirable outcome is indeterminate, being a function of whatever desires people happen to have. The question here is this: is the economic justification for democracy as conceived by the economic theorists a sound one?

This question is a fundamental one for democratic theory. Notions like self-government, autonomy, and popular sovereignty have occupied a central position in other theories of democracy we have discussed. One impulse behind the theories emphasizing participation discussed in Chapter III seems to be the idea that popular participation in government constitutes a kind of self rule. In Chapter IV I discussed the idea that democratic government preserves the autonomy of citizens by legislating in accordance with something called the will of the people. The economic theories discussed in this chapter again seem to incorporate a conception of self government, but here the model is that of an efficient (Pareto optimal) allocation of resources preserving something like the kind of consumer sovereignty that one supposedly finds in the free market. The idea is that government should respond to people's tastes and desires in the way that the market responds to the tastes and desires of consumers.

If we understand self government in terms of popular participation there are some questions about the long term stability of a system of self government, but on the whole self government seems to be a feasible ideal. However, self government, so understood, is not obviously desirable. It certainly is not self justifying. Given a coherent conception of the people's will satisfying certain conditions it might seem that a government designed to accord with that will would be self justifying. The problem is that there does not seem to be any such conception of the people's will. The economic theory of democracy, on the other hand, seems to offer an account of self government that is both feasible and also has a certain amount of justificatory force. Moreover, it would seem that any conception of *democracy* must permit at least something like this kind of self rule. Nevertheless, it seems to me that this kind of self rule is not sufficient to justify the system. When we evaluate legislation or policy from a moral point of view, we must reject some laws or policies even when they reflect the tastes or desires of individuals in the way we are considering. Indeed, it could be argued that we must sometimes reject these laws just because they are responses to desires – the *wrong* desires. What I have just said might be disputed. Bentham, defending utility or satisfaction of desire as the criterion of moral rightness, says that it is only on principles contrary to that of utility '. . . that the most abominable pleasure which the vilest of malefactors ever reaped from his crime would be to be reprobated, if it stood alone'.[5] According to the principle of utility, any pleasure, other things equal, is to be satisfied; any desire constitutes a prima facie moral claim for satisfaction. It is only when the pleasure derived from the satisfaction of one kind of desire gives rise to pain or frustration of other desires that there is any reason not to satisfy it – and then only when the pain outweighs the pleasure. Now democracy, as conceived by the economic theorists, does tend to satisfy people's desires and it even responds to differences in intensity of desire. At least roughly speaking, then, a utilitarian might regard the economic conception of self rule as sufficient to justify a system embodying that conception of self rule. Does this just show what is wrong with utilitarianism as a moral theory?

Suppose society contains a racial minority and suppose that the majority is bigoted. Among the desires of the majority is a desire to isolate the racial minority in ghettos and deprive them of access to various social advantages. Should social policy reflect the preferences of the majority at all? If so, to what extent and in what way? If democracy works as the economic theorists think, it will adopt laws and policies reflecting the preferences of the majority, though it will not necessarily neglect completely the interests of the minority. A number of variables will affect the outcome. In a system requiring unanimous consensus for action, segregationist policies may be adopted, but only if the minority willingly goes along, which will presumably require that they be compensated in other ways. In a system of majority rule permitting buying and selling of votes, the outcome will depend on such factors as the resources of the minority – how many votes they can buy – which will in turn depend on the strength of preference of members of the majority. Even without formal vote buying, much will depend on the precise pattern of overlapping interest groups. For example, if some members of the majority have a relatively weak interest in segregation, but share some strong preference with members of the racial minority, we may have the kind of situation discussed earlier in this chapter in which a coalition of minorities would be able to defeat a party espousing the majority position on the single issue of segregation. Obviously there are many possibilities, and majority tyranny is not bound to occur. Every sinister interest will not prevail, but, of course, neither will every virtuous interest. Every interest, whether sinister or virtuous, has a potential effect. This fact, in my view, is sufficient to raise serious questions about the desirability of democracy as conceived by the economic theorists. Perhaps it is sufficient to raise serious questions about any conception of democracy if democracy requires self government and if that in turn requires that we take citizens' preferences as given and adopt legislation that somehow reflects these preferences.

Most of us, I believe, do not now hold that all desires and all preferences are intrinsically worthy of satisfaction. We distinguish among desires on grounds other than mere strength or intensity when these desires are presented as the basis for a moral claim.[16] We are likely to overlook this point because usually, when we are called upon to adjudicate disputes, competing desires do represent legitimate claims; and frequently they are *otherwise* on a par so that intensity is the only relevant consideration. But there are cases — extreme avarice, perhaps, or bigotry — where most of us probably hold that the preferences in question should, at the very least, be given less weight in our deliberations regardless of their degree of intensity. If this is right, our morality has a structure more complicated than the structure suggested by utilitarianism. Whether it should have this structure is another question. If it should, then the desirability of democracy as understood by the economic theorists must remain in doubt.

CONCLUSIONS

Since Chapter III I have argued that a justification of democracy requires a conception of what democracy is together with a demonstration that democracy so conceived is at least as likely as any other kind of system to produce morally acceptable legislation. The theories discussed in Chapters II and III largely ignored evaluations of the likely outcomes of the democratic process. The theories discussed in Chapter IV were concerned with outcomes, but what they demanded of outcomes is of dubious moral value, and, in any case, seems to represent an unfeasible goal. The economic theorists discussed in the present chapter are seriously concerned to predict the likely results of democratic politics; and insofar as they are concerned with justification, they would argue for democracy by reference to its consequences. Though their approach is more formal, their conclusions about the nature of the system are not unlike the conclusions of political scientists who see democratic politics as a system for adjudicating among and responding to the demands of shifting pressure groups in a pluralistic society.[17] But while their attempt to understand and evaluate the system in terms of its consequences represents, in my view, an appropriate approach to democratic theory, I believe it has not yielded an adequate moral justification for the system. Either they have ignored features of systems like ours that have significant effects on the range of likely outcomes, or we must redefine democracy, or democracy is not a particularly good form of government.

93

VI

OPEN GOVERNMENT AND JUST LEGISLATION: A DEFENSE OF DEMOCRACY

It is important to bear in mind the distinctions between the different parts of a complete theory of democracy. To reject a theory on the ground that the system it proposes is unfeasible, for example, is not necessarily to deny that it is an inspiring ideal. More important, to reject a theory on the ground that it embodies an inadequate justification of a system of democracy is not to deny the possibility that democracy, as defined, *can* be justified — that there are other good arguments in its favor. Thus, while I have criticized a number of theories of democracy, I have not said that there is no adequate theory. Indeed, I have not even denied that democracy, as defined in one of the theories I have criticized, might be given an adequate justification. With the exception of the theory of democracy as popular sovereignty, which I rejected partly on grounds of feasibility, I have objected to various theories primarily because of the justifications they embody. Before turning to my positive tasks in this chapter, I shall take another brief look at some of these criticisms.

My main point could be summarized in this way: none of the theories discussed in Chapters II, III or V take the problem of justifying democracy seriously enough. The theories discussed in these chapters all assume the desirability of what they are supposed to be justifying. Now, this way of putting my point is itself misleading, but I hope it is also illuminating. Consider the argument from fairness discussed in Chapter II. To be sure, it is possible to offer a characterization of democracy in terms of majority rule and to argue for this system in terms of the further claim that majority rule distributes political power equally. To argue thus is not to claim that democracy, as characterized, is self justifying. Majority rule is justified only because it distributes power fairly and equally. But it would not seem particularly odd if someone were to *define* democracy as the type of system that distributes power equally. If the argument from fairness were an adequate justification for democracy, then, on at least one not unreasonable characterization of democracy, democracy *would* be self justifying. To put the point another way: when people ask whether democracy is a desirable system, precisely what they mean to ask, at least sometimes, is whether it is desirable that political power be distributed equally.

What I have just said about the argument from fairness could also be said about the economic justification of democracy. Here again, the kind of theory I have actually discussed characterizes democracy in terms of certain voting rules and procedures and then goes on to argue that a government ought to operate according to these rules and procedures because of their predicted results. However, the result which is assumed desirable in this argument, namely, maximum feasible satisfaction of whatever desires people happen to have ('consumer sovereignty' for the consumers of government's products), is just the kind of goal that people often mean to be questioning when they question the value of democracy. More important, it seems to me not unreasonable to question the desirability of the democratic goals in terms of which both the argument from fairness and the economic argument propose that we justify democracy. It does not seem wildly unreasonable to suggest that not all desires deserve satisfaction and that some desires do not even deserve to be taken into account. For related reasons, it does not seem unreasonable at least to question the idea that political power should be shared equally by everyone.

The theories that cluster around the idea of maximum political participation or the idea of a participatory society present a more complex picture. Some versions seem to define democracy in terms of participation and then do little more than assert that people have a right to participate or that participation is intrinsically desirable. Some versions argue for participation in terms of its effects, but the effects in question are simply the long term stability of the participatory system – hardly an independent justification of the system! But some versions of participation theory suggest that participation has beneficial effects on the moral quality both of citizens and governmental policy. This kind of argument was never fully developed by the theorists considered in Chapter III, but it does at least deserve further consideration.

What we need to do, if we are to offer an argument for democracy

95

capable of convincing those who are not already convinced democrats, is to begin with an independent account of what is morally desirable and why it is morally desirable. If we can then argue, in terms of such an account, that democracy is desirable itself, or has desirable consequences, we will have made some progress. This is what I shall attempt to do in this chapter. The task will require an excursion into moral theory, and then a discussion of how a representative democracy might be expected to work so as to produce government acceptable from the perspective of the kind of moral theory I shall sketch. Following this discussion I shall return once again to the theories I have discussed in earlier chapters in order to explore the similarities and differences between my own theory and these alternatives.

The theory I shall develop in this chapter will be an instrumental theory. I shall argue that democracy is desirable largely because of its good effects — because it tends to produce good laws and policies, or, at least, to prevent bad ones. But this kind of theory has been subjected to serious criticism, perhaps most notably by Robert Dahl in his widely read *Preface to Democratic Theory*.[1] Since some of Dahl's arguments can be taken to be general arguments against any justification of the type I shall attempt, I must discuss Dahl's critique of Madison before proceeding with the program I have outlined.

1 DAHL ON MADISON

The first chapter of *Preface to Democratic Theory* is a critique of what Dahl takes to be the Madisonian theory of democracy. Democracy, on this theory, is American constitutional democracy with its complex system of checks on the power of majorities. Madison's argument for this system, according to Dahl, is that a republican form of government, circumscribed by checks on the power of majorities, is necessary to prevent tyranny. The absence of either popular elections or constitutional checks and balances will lead to tyranny (Dahl, 11).[2] This is a justification of constitutional democracy in terms of its substantive effects, and Dahl argues that it fails. He criticizes it on two grounds. First, assuming that we know what tyranny is, Dahl argues that Madison's justification seems to be based on a false empirical generalization. Second, he argues that we cannot really even test this generalization since we cannot give an adequate account of what tyranny is. True, we could define 'tyranny' in such a way that any nonrepublican government

or government without separation of powers, was, by definition, tyran-
nical. But that kind of definition makes the argument trivial and unin-
teresting. The argument is interesting only if we begin with an independent definition of 'tyranny', but no such definition is adequate.

The first objection presupposes that the second is mistaken, so it is
hard to see just how we are to take it. Still, it seems reasonable to say
that, on any initially plausible account of tyranny, there are possible
nontyrannical governments that lack the kind of constitutional restraints
on the power of majorities that we find in the United States Constitution. Great Britain is a good enough example (Dahl, 13). Moreover,
common sense, together with a good deal of social theory, suggests that
noninstitutional, psychological restraints can be just as effective as legal
restraints in preventing abuse of power (Dahl, 17-19).[3] So, it seems
doubtful that a constitutional democracy of the sort Madison had in
mind is necessary to prevent tyranny.

The second objection is the more fundamental one. If it is successful, it will undermine any attempt to justify a system of government by
reference to a substantive moral goal like the avoidance of tyranny.
How exactly does the objection go? To define 'tyranny' in terms of the
deprivation of natural rights is not to define it adequately unless we can
'specify a process by which specific natural rights can be defined in the
context of some political society' (Dahl, 23). Any attempt to do so in a
way consistent with other elements of a theory like Madison's will fail,
so, 'tyranny seems to have no operational meaning in the context of
political decision-making' (Dahl, 24). Now, the general point here presumably is not limited to definitions of 'tyranny' or definitions of
'natural rights'. The point, rather, is that a justification of a form of
government based on the claim that that government will produce certain kinds of legislation requires a precise account of the kind of legislation in question. Otherwise, it will be impossible to determine the truth
of the key premise in the argument. Dahl thinks he has an argument to
rule out any adequate account, but I believe his argument fails.

There are two problems with Dahl's argument. First, he demands
more of an adequate definition than he needs to demand, and, second,
even given his overly strong requirement, he fails to demonstrate that it
cannot be met. The second point is the easier one to make. Dahl argues
by elimination. He considers only three possible theories of natural
rights: that each person has a right to do whatever he wants; that each
has a right to do whatever is not unanimously condemned; and, that
each has a right to do whatever is not condemned by a majority. Dahl

97

holds each of these theories to be either impractical or inconsistent with other elements of a theory like Madison's. (The third, for example, seems to rule out the possibility of majority tyranny (Dahl, 23-4).) But these are not all the possible theories of natural rights; so we cannot conclude that there is *no* adequate theory. And what a strange collection of theories Dahl has chosen to discuss! Moral theorists do not generally take seriously accounts of moral rights that make those rights depend on how people happen to vote. (What if they are immoral?) But here Dahl seems to be a victim of his decision to require not just a clear and precise account of the ethical goals to be attained by the political process, but an account that determines, *by some decisive political process*, what those goals involve. This brings us back to the first of the two problems mentioned above: Dahl demands more of an adequate definition than he needs to demand.

At the very least, Dahl requires that a definition of natural rights be operational. There are serious philosophical problems about the requirement of operational definition in any area of inquiry.[4] But, even if we assume that something like the requirement of operational definition is reasonable, I think Dahl requires too much. Everyone would agree, I suppose, that reasonable clarity and precision is desirable. No doubt one idea associated with operational definition is just this idea. The proponents of operational definition want to be able to say what does and does not follow from this or that proposition — what its truth conditions are. But they also want the presence or absence of these truth conditions to be subject to public determination. They want an account of truth conditions such that there will be virtually no room for disagreement about whether or not they are satisfied. Most would agree, however, that verifiability *in principle* is the most we can require. The most we can require is that, for each proposition, if we had the time, resources and so on, we could get near universal agreement on the truth or falsity of the proposition. Consider, for example, the concepts that figured in the economic analyses of democracy discussed in the preceding chapter, concepts like 'Pareto optimality' and 'Pareto improvement'. Even supposing a reasonable operational account of 'P prefers x to y', it would be virtually impossible to determine in an actual case whether one situation was really Pareto better than another. Yet the notion of a Pareto improvement is generally conceded to be the kind of notion that satisfies reasonable requirements of operationality.[5] Dahl, however, wants more than this.

If we want a political system that will make laws, if we want these laws to be an effective determinant of conduct, and if we want to penalize those who violate the laws, we need clear criteria, about which there can be little disagreement, by means of which we can determine what the law requires and who has complied with it. It is not enough that this be determinable merely *in principle*. We need procedures that will terminate in a reasonably short period of time. When we attach practical consequences to the truth or falsity of certain propositions, we need practical, decisive procedures by which to determine their truth or falsity. Dahl, I want to suggest, confuses the requirement of decisive procedures appropriate in political contexts with the weaker requirements of clarity and verifiability in principle which may be appropriate in some theoretical contexts. It is for this reason that Dahl considers only accounts of natural rights stated in terms of procedures like majority rule.

I do not want to deny the importance of decisive, practical procedures in political systems. The question how we should go about justifying our choice of procedures is an important one just because we need some procedures. It is a difficult question just because no procedure can capture the moral criteria by which we evaluate political decisions. But the question whether a given system or procedure is justified is not itself a political question; it is a theoretical question. We do not need a decisive procedure to settle the question of the justifiability of our political decision procedures. Still, if we are to defend democracy, as Madison evidently did, by arguing that it tends to have results of a certain kind, it is incumbent on us to give a reasonably clear account of the kind of result we have in mind. To this extent, I agree with Dahl. But when Dahl objects that there is no way to clarify Madison's goal of nontyranny, he bases his objection on a survey of an absurdly small and irrelevant sample of possible attempts to clarify this goal. Apparently, this is because he requires more than clarity, and more even than what is normally demanded by those who require operational definitions.

Conceivably, Dahl was dimly aware of this kind of problem when he allowed himself to assume, at the beginning of his discussion of Madison, that we do have a clear enough understanding of what constitutes tyranny to evaluate Madison's central empirical claim — the claim that republican government with separation of powers is necessary for nontyrannical government. Dahl thinks it obvious, indeed, that there are governments significantly different from Madison's constitutional democracy that nevertheless manage to be nontyrannical. But now we should look again at this criticism. I do not want to quibble about the interpretation of Madison's writings in *The Federalist*; but, clearly, some theories *like* the theory Dahl attributes to Madison are immune to Dahl's criticisms. Thus, one might argue for some form of constitutional democracy not on the ground that it is *necessary* for decent government, but on the ground that it is more likely than other forms of government to lead to decent government. In sum, then, Dahl's arguments fall far short of ruling out any attempt to justify democracy in terms of the moral quality of its likely substantive results.

2 MORALITY AND JUST GOVERNMENT

The most important question about the system of laws and institutions making up the state is whether they satisfy the conditions morality lays down for such systems. Morality determines the limits of the permissible for systems of laws and institutions as well as for individual conduct. It has been said that 'justice is the first virtue of institutions'.[6] If this is so, it is so because a reasonable moral theory assigns a kind of priority to considerations of justice or because, in such a theory, considerations referred to as considerations of justice are just those relevant to the assessment of institutions. I have no objection to this way of speaking, but it leaves us with the following question: when it is true that legal, political or economic institutions are just, what does this involve? This is a substantive moral question. It can be answered only within a substantive theory. I shall argue for democracy, here, on the ground that it tends to produce specific laws and policies that are just. I am assuming that this kind of argument is sufficient to justify a political system, or at least to create a strong presumption in its favor. Suppose someone says that this kind of argument is irrelevant — that the crucial question concerns not the effects of the system, but its intrinsic features, whether it is fair, for example. I have no *general* argument against this position. I have attempted to reply to specific theories of this type in earlier chapters. I hope to establish, in this chapter, at least the possibility of a coherent, plausible justification in terms of effects. Skepticism about the possibility of such a theory, as voiced by Dahl for example, may well be one reason for the prevalence of 'procedural' theories.

If we are to argue that democracy satisfies principles of justice, and if this requires us to argue that democracy is well designed to produce just laws and policies, we clearly must say something about what justice, and morality in general, require. One way to carry out a defense of democracy along these lines would be this: offer an account of which laws are morally good laws, and then try to show that democracies tend to have good laws and that other governments do not. (Dahl used something analogous to this procedure to discredit Madison's contention that democracy is necessary for good government.) There are other possibilities, however. When Buchanan and Tullock argue that certain kinds of democratic procedure will lead to Pareto optimal outcomes, or to Pareto improvements on the status quo, they do not proceed by examining governments of various kinds and establishing correlations. Instead, they begin with a reasonably precise, abstract specification of the goals to be achieved and of the system they have in mind, and then, given more or less standard motivational assumptions, *deduce* the consequence they seek from their definitions, assumptions and certain well-known results in economic theory. Of course, their argument is not as formal as I make it sound here, and my argument will not be as formal as theirs; but my argument will be more like theirs than like the other alternative mentioned. The mechanics of democracy are such, I shall argue, that, given certain assumptions about human nature, democracy will automatically tend to produce morally acceptable results. Now this kind of argument, like the others I have mentioned, seems to presuppose a clear account of which laws are morally good laws. I shall have something to say along these lines, but most of my argument will proceed at a higher level of abstraction. Instead of offering anything like a complete account of what morality requires, I shall suggest an account of what a (reasonable) morality is. This account will embody conditions which must be satisfied by any acceptable moral principles. I shall then argue that, following the procedures of (a kind of) constitutional democracy, we will tend to come up with laws that are justifiable in terms of principles satisfying the conditions of acceptability for moral principles. The general idea is this: the tests that a law has to pass to be adopted in a constitutional democracy are analogous to the tests that a moral principle must pass in order to be an acceptable moral principle.

What conditions must a principle satisfy in order to be an acceptable moral principle? What conditions must a set of principles satisfy if they are to constitute an adequate morality? What principles are true moral principles? It is natural to think that the answer to these questions depends on an account of the function of morality: true moral principles are principles that perform the function of moral principles. Looking at the problem in this way generates difficult questions. If two distinct sets of principles would equally well perform the function of morality, for example, is each set a set of true principles? More fundamental, however, is the question whether there is any such thing as *the* function(s) of morality. And how do we know when we have found it (them)? I do not have definitive answers to these questions. Nevertheless, I shall propose an account of morality in terms of its functions. The account I offer is not the only possible account of its kind. Others have been, or might be, offered. But neither is my account idiosyncratic. My suggestions about the function of morality should seem familiar both to theorists (since it is borrowed from other theorists) and to ordinary people. I think they are plausible suggestions. More important, whether or not what I offer here correctly captures the 'essence' of morality seems to me *relatively* unimportant. What is more important is that we have reason to be interested in morality as I conceive it. The functions of morality, on my account, are important functions. We have reason to be interested in principles or rules performing these functions, and we have reason to be interested in the truth or falsity of judgments made with respect to these rules. In any case, I believe it is better to leave off these preliminary discussions and turn to the account itself. We will be in a better position to decide what to do with the account when we have it before us.

3 A CONCEPTION OF MORALITY

Minimally, a morality can be described by a system of rules or principles proscribing some kinds of harmful or dangerous conduct and enjoining certain kinds of beneficial conduct. Such rules constitute a system of constraints or boundaries determining the limits of the permissible. To speak of these rules as constraints is to emphasize their overriding character; when moral considerations conflict with other considerations, moral considerations take precedence. Moral rules, as so far described, can be usefully distinguished into two groups. (1) Some rules proscribe or enjoin actions that are either harmful or useful in themselves, regardless of what other people are doing; (2) Some rules enjoin actions which will either prevent harm or promote benefits just in case they are generally performed.[7] Rules of type (2) may be either direct rules, enjoining specific types of conduct, or indirect rules requiring simply that people adhere to whatever specific rules or conventions are being generally adhered to.[8] When I speak here of rules governing actions, I include actions establishing or altering institutional structures. When I speak of rules requiring that we benefit or refrain from harming people, I do not mean to exclude rules requiring that we benefit some at the expense of others. Thus, moral rules can include rules for settling disputes when one gains only at the expense of another, and they can also include rules governing the distribution or redistribution of goods.

Even if any morality includes rules of the sort described here, it does not follow that such rules exhaust the content of morality, nor, more importantly, does it mean that any such set of rules constitutes an *adequate* morality. What more is necessary? Let me begin by considering John Rawls's notion of a 'well-ordered society'. A society is well-ordered, he says, when it is 'effectively regulated by a public conception of justice'. More specifically, '(1) everyone accepts and knows that the others accept, the same principles of justice, and (2) the basic social institutions generally satisfy and are generally known to satisfy these principles'. In a well-ordered society, 'while men may put forth excessive demands on one another, they nevertheless acknowledge a common point of view from which their claims may be adjudicated'. The shared, public system of principles constitutes 'the fundamental charter of a well-ordered human association'.[9]

Pretty clearly, the notion of a well-ordered society admits of degrees. Consensus on principles can be more or less perfect, and institutions can vary in the degree to which they satisfy the conditions layed down in the shared moral principles. In a perfectly well-ordered society, though, there will be complete agreement on principles for evaluating actions and common institutions. Moreover, I take it, there will be agreement that these principles are final (Rawls, 135-6). These principles are the *fundamental charter* of a well-ordered association. When these principles apply to a specific decision, they are taken to override any other considerations that might also apply. Thus, the shared, public system of rules in a well-ordered society plays the same role in the life of the community earlier assigned to moral rules in general. It is regarded as a system of *constraints* determining the limits of the permissible.

When a proposal is agreed to be contrary to the shared system of principles, it will be rejected by all. On the other hand, there may well be disagreement about the acceptability, *all things considered*, of proposals consistent with the shared morality. Nor is this the only source of disagreement and strife. While there is agreement, in a well-ordered society, on fundamental principles, there may not be agreement on the

103

consequences of their application to particular cases. Typically, there will be agreement on what is relevant to a given decision, but there may well be disagreement on the truth or falsity of some statement that all regard as relevant. Nevertheless, the knowledge that there is agreement on ends strengthens 'the bonds of civic friendship' (Rawls, 5), and mitigates the otherwise devisive effects of disagreement on specific matters of policy.

I want to suggest that one important function of a morality is to serve as the public system of constraints on action agreed to by citizens in a well-ordered society. A test for an *adequate* morality is that its principles be able to perform this function. The more stable a system of principles — the greater its capacity to continue to perform this function as a society grows and changes — the more adequate it is.

In general, then, those parts of a morality relevant to the assessment of laws and institutions consist of a system of final rules compliance with which tends to prevent harm or produce benefits. An adequate morality is a system of such rules on which there could be an enduring consensus. It is a system of rules that could be accepted by all members of society as principles determining the absolute limits of the permissible. Now, the idea of focusing on what could be agreed to or on what could constitute a consensus is like the idea that seems to underlie much moral theory in the social contract tradition.[10] There are, of course, differences within that tradition. Some theorists, for example, see moral principles as principles that *would* be agreed to in more or less idealized situations. Others hold that moral principles are principles actually agreed to in actual situations. The position I have sketched here is like those theories emphasizing hypothetical agreement since it asserts that an adequate morality is a system of principles that could be accepted by everyone, even if none is accepted now. On the other hand, it is like theories emphasizing an actual agreement in that it says a morality constitutes a possible consensus among actual people. There is precedent for this kind of combination. Indeed, I believe there is a plausible interpretation of Rawls's contract theory in which the notion of a well-ordered society plays the central role it plays in mine. On this reading of Rawls, a morality (or, anyway, principles of justice) constitutes a possible, public conception of justice in a well-ordered society. The appeal to the original contract — to the 'original position' in Rawls's theory — is designed to establish the *possibility* of consensus on principles of justice. When we find out that people in the original position would agree to certain principles, we find out that consensus, at least for a time, among some people, is possible. When we find out what they would agree to, we find out something about what kind of principles might form the basis of an *enduring* consensus. Principles people would agree to, in an initial situation of equality, behind a veil of ignorance, will be the kind of principles they would continue to accept in spite of changes in their prospects or other circumstances. But *full* justification of moral principles, on this interpretation, requires more than a demonstration that these principles would be chosen in the original position. It requires a demonstration that people in real societies are, or could become, sufficiently like people in the original position that principles chosen by the latter people could constitute a consensus among the former.[11]

One way in which my theory resembles other contract theories is that it seems to be subject to some of the same criticisms. Consider this question: why should we believe that real people ought to comply with the principles that ideal people would agree to in some hypothetical situation? This objection corresponds to the question about my theory, why should we believe that people ought to comply with rules that could, or even do, constitute a consensus on fundamental constraints on conduct? This question could be interpreted in different ways. (1) It might be the question whether we have any reason to be interested in the requirements of such systems of rules. (2) It could be the question whether what people would agree to has anything to do with what *morality* requires of them, or (3) it could be the question how, logically speaking, we can *derive* an 'ought' judgment from the mere existence of some system of principles or rules. To this last question, I believe, the most plausible response is in terms of something like the theory of 'ought' judgments developed by Roger Wertheimer in *The Significance of Sense*.[12] According to Wertheimer, roughly, all 'ought' judgments refer implicity to some system of rules or principles. To say that *x* ought to do *y* is to say: (1) There is an adequate and relevant system of rules; (2) According to some rule of that system, were *x* in some situation *s*, *x* would (ideally or actually) *y*; and (3) *x* is in situation *s*. A system is a relevant system if it is a system of the type to which the speaker means to refer. It is an adequate system if it satisfies the conditions of adequacy for systems of its type.[13] Now, given an account of 'ought' judgments along these lines, there is no particular logical problem about how we could derive such judgments, given a system of rules of the sort discussed here. But do we have reason to be interested in rules that constitute a possible consensus, and would those rules be adequate moral rules? I shall comment first on the latter question and then turn to the former.

I have suggested that we think of a morality as a system of overriding constraints on action compliance with which tends to produce benefits or prevent harm and which could serve as the fundamental charter of a well-ordered society. I have not said that any system of rules with these two properties is an adequate morality. The properties mentioned are necessary conditions. Are there other necessary conditions? The question whether the rules imagined here would be a morality no doubt stems partly from the feeling that the class of acceptable rules needs to be narrowed down further. At the very least, one might say, a set of principles is an adequate morality only when it represents a possible consensus *among free and independent persons*. We could imagine a kind of slave society in which the slaves themselves are so dehumanized that they would accept the slaveholders' rationale for their common institutions. But, given the modification suggested here, that would not show that these institutions were morally acceptable. To show this, we would have to show that principles permitting such institutions *would* be acceptable to all concerned even if they were free from its dehumanizing effects.

The requirement that a set of principles be a potential *stable* consensus — a consensus that would endure over time — will tend to rule out some seemingly unfair sets of principles in some societies. When there is social mobility, so that any person (or any person's child) might occupy most any position in society, people will be reluctant to accept principles giving special, permanent advantages even to their own social class. And, if they do, consensus on those principles will tend to break down as people who have known those advantages come to occupy less advantageous positions. However, in a rigid caste society, we would find neither of these kinds of check on the adoption of principles that look grossly unfair. A caste society with a caste morality may be a stable, well-ordered society. It does make some difference, then, whether we make it a necessary condition for a morality's being adequate that it constitute a possible, stable consensus among free and independent persons. But should we say this?

I shall argue here that people generally have reason to promote and comply with principles satisfying the conditions I have so far laid down; and I shall argue that people generally have a greater interest in such principles when those principles would be acceptable under conditions of freedom and independence. I do not believe this is a *proof* that principles satisfying the conditions in question constitute an adequate morality. If one holds that, by definition, moral principles are principles on which people have a reason to act, then my argument is relevant to such a proof. Be that as it may, the argument does serve as a partial justification of the kind of principles I have in mind, at least to those who share a certain ideal of social cooperation. Moreover, if I am correct, morality as I conceive it can perform what might be regarded as one of its characteristic functions: people can successfully appeal to its principles in order to criticize the conduct of others or to justify their own.[14]

With or without the added requirement that principles be acceptable to free and independent persons, what reason do we have to take an interest in moral principles as described here? Suppose, to begin with, that we are in a well-ordered society. If so, there will be a set of fundamental principles on which people agree, and it will be agreed that these principles determine the limits of the permissible. They entail a set of constraints on conduct within which, it is agreed, we must confine ourselves. They will require that we refrain from harming one another in various ways, and they will require that we benefit one another in various ways. Also, in a well-ordered society, legal, political and economic institutions will be justifiable from the perspective of these shared principles, and it will be agreed that this is so. Now, on these assumptions, we will want others to comply with our shared principles insofar as we stand to benefit (or to avoid harm) as a result of their compliance. More interesting, it will generally be in the interest of each individual to conform to those shared principles himself and to develop the general disposition to do so. It will also generally be in the interest of each that basic institutions continue to be justifiable in terms of the society's shared principles. The argument for these conclusions is pretty straightforward. Given a general belief in certain fundamental constraints, and given a normal interest in the opinions of others, each will want to *appear* to limit his behavior by those constraints. But the easiest way to appear to conform to principles, usually, is to conform to them! And, if one has an interest in such general conformity, one has an interest in developing the general disposition to conform. Moreover, given an interest in conforming to shared principles, each has an interest in minimizing conflict between the requirements of these principles and the constraints and requirements of institutions. When one benefits from institutional constraints on others, one wants to be able to justify those constraints. When one is able to make use of institutions to his advantage, one wants to be able to justify one's conduct to others. All this requires, however, that the institutions themselves be justifiable in terms of shared, public principles.

In a well-ordered society, under plausible assumptions about human motives, people generally have a reason to conform to shared principles of morality. Do they have *more* reason to conform to principles acceptable to free and independent persons than to principles that are not? Most people are concerned about the opinions of others, and this concern, at the very least, makes them want to appear to conform to shared principles. The reasons for this will vary from person to person. Some, perhaps, will simply want to avoid criticism. Even then, they will do well to cultivate a general disposition to conform, since actual conformity virtually guarantees the appearance of conformity, and alternative strategies can involve costly calculation and planning. But most of us, to a greater or lesser degree, do not want merely to appear to comply with generally accepted standards. We want, in Philippa Foot's nice phrase, 'to live openly and in good faith with [our] neighbors'.[15] Not only do we want to avoid the consequences of hypocrisy (always being on guard, trying to keep our lies consistent and so on), but we find lying and deceit intrinsically unpleasant. We do not want to have to conceal; we want our lives to be able to stand inspection. All this, of course, strictly requires only that we comply with whatever restrictions people actually believe in. But if it makes us feel uncomfortable to have to conceal our conduct from others, it will hardly satisfy us to know that we can justify our conduct to others only because they have come to accept certain principles under duress or some psychological constraint. At least the latter attitude seems a natural extension of the former. For many of us, then, some of the same considerations that lead us to take an interest in the requirements of shared principles will lead us also to take a greater interest in requirements that would be acceptable to people choosing freely and independently.

I have argued so far only that people in a well-ordered society have a reason to comply with generally accepted principles. But I have said that a morality consists of a set of principles that *would* perform the function of the public conception of justice in a well-ordered society. Do we have a reason to take an interest in a morality — in principles that would serve this function — when we are not in a well-ordered society? Does this property of a morality give us a reason to take an interest in it when it is not generally accepted? Most of us, I think, do have a reason to want principles to be generally accepted, and to comply with principles that could be generally accepted even when no such principles are now accepted. So long as we wish to be able to justify our conduct to others, we have reason to comply with rules that others *could* be led to accept; we also have reason to try to get those principles accepted. To this point, the argument is like the argument for comply-ing with rules actually accepted in a well-ordered society. But suppose many people accept principles — racist principles might be an example — that are *inconsistent* with principles that could be generally accepted. In this case, conduct that *could* be justified to everyone, in the long run, could not be justified to many people in the short run. In this kind of situation, it is far from clear that individuals have a reason to care about what morality requires. At least, whether a given person has reason to act according to principles that could be generally accepted will depend to a far greater extent on particular motives and features of his situation that are likely to differ from those of others. It will depend on the extent to which he must deal with members of racial minorities, for example; and it will depend on whether his desire to be able to justify his conduct to others is based on a mere desire to avoid ostracism and reprisals, or on a respect for persons as persons.

Aside from the desire to be able to justify our conduct to others, it should be remembered, we have other reasons to want certain kinds of general principles adopted and complied with. According to the theory under consideration, a morality is not just any system of principles that can be generally accepted and publicly avowed. It is a system of princi-ples requiring some beneficial conduct and proscribing some harmful conduct. But then, insofar as we stand to benefit (or avoid harm) from compliance on the part of others, we have reason to want them to comply. Thus, we have an additional, independent reason to push for the acceptance of principles that could gain general acceptance and that people could therefore have a reason to comply with. One reason people have for complying with rules depends on the acceptability of those rules to other people. So, our interest in compliance on the part of others also gives us an interest in the general acceptability of those rules. It leads us to try to find systems of constraints that are, intuitively speaking, fair as well as beneficial.

Let me summarize. An adequate morality, I have suggested, can be described by a set of principles or rules having, at least, the following properties: (1) Compliance with the principles tends to produce bene-fits or prevent harm; (2) The principles could serve as the shared, public principles constituting a stable, 'fundamental charter of a well-ordered human association' as Rawls understands this notion; and (3) The principles could perform this function in a society of free and independent persons. The idea is that it is a necessary condition for a system's being an adequate morality that it satisfy these conditions, but I did not argue for this conclusion directly. What I argued is that we have reason to want *some* such set of principles accepted and generally complied with. If some set is accepted and complied with, we have reason to comply ourselves and to urge continued compliance on the part of others. We have reason to treat them with the seriousness normally accorded a morality.

It should be emphasized that the arguments in this section depend on empirical assumptions, and that the conclusions hold only other things being equal. First, the arguments depend clearly on assumptions about human motives and interests, like the assumption that we are not generally indifferent to the opinions of others; and they depend on assumptions about our circumstances, like the assumption that it is costly and difficult to conceal one's conduct. These assumptions *could* be false, but I think they are not. Second, the extent to which one has a reason to comply with the directives of morality (as conceived here) will depend on the extent to which others accept and comply with those directives. If no one accepted principles with the properties of an adequate morality, people would have much less reason to try to develop and comply with such principles. Still, it is hard to imagine a complete lack of consensus on principles within subgroups in a society anyhow; and, in the absence of a rigid caste structure, people would tend to comply with principles most widely accepted and therefore most widely acceptable. The long run tendency is toward general compliance with, and general acceptance of, principles that have the properties of an adequate morality. But, even if this is right, it does not follow at all that each person will always have an overriding reason to comply with such principles in particular cases.[16]

At the beginning of the section before this one, I asked what conditions a political system had to satisfy in order to be morally acceptable, and I said that this question is itself a substantive moral question. In this section, I have offered a partial account of the nature of an adequate morality, but I have said virtually nothing about its substantive content. If I am right, of course, the substantive requirements of morality will depend on what kinds of principles people can agree to under certain conditions and for certain purposes. What I shall argue in the next two sections is that familiar institutions of representative democracy tend to foster consensus on adequate principles of morality, and consequently tend to produce law and policy decisions consistent with these principles. The argument will depend in part on the precise nature of representative institutions and it will also presuppose some of the motivational assumptions I have introduced in this section in arguing that people have reason to care about the requirements of an adequate morality. The idea that this argument constitutes a *justification* for democracy depends on an assumption about what the substantive requirements of an adequate morality would be. Specifically, I assume that an adequate morality will include requirements that laws and social policy must satisfy, and I assume that it will not require anything of political decision procedures other than that they tend to produce acceptable laws and policies.

4 DEMOCRACY AND JUST GOVERNMENT: MILL'S ARGUMENT

In this section I shall offer an interpretation and defense of the theory of democracy John Stuart Mill presented in *Considerations on Representative Government.*[17] I think Mill's justification of representative government is, in its main lines, reasonable. Other philosophers have suggested similar arguments, and Mill's argument needs to be supplemented at certain points; but I shall begin with Mill here, partly because he has sometimes been misinterpreted, and partly because, properly interpreted, he makes the case about as well as anyone.

According to Mill, the 'ideally best form of government', the 'form of government most eligible in itself', is representative government (Mill, 35-6). What does Mill mean by 'most eligible in itself', and what, in his view, are the criteria for good government in general? Basic to Mill's theory of government is the idea that different systems of government are appropriate in different societies and in different stages in the development of a given society. The form of government ideally best in itself, then, is not the form of government best under all circumstances. Instead, the idea is this: We consider all possible states of society, and we suppose that each is governed by the form of government best for that state of society. Each form of government, then, is operating in its most propitious circumstances, and we say that the society that is best governed has the form of government that is best in itself. In Mill's words, that government is 'most eligible in itself ... which, if the necessary conditions existed for giving effect to its beneficial tendencies,

111

would, more than all others, favor and promote not some one improvement, but all forms and degrees of it' (Mill, 35).

That form of government is best in itself which, given propitious circumstances, has the best effects. Government, according to Mill, is a *means* to certain ends (Mill, 15). But to what ends? What is the function of government? In Mill's view, there are two *criteria* for a good government. On the one hand, government must 'promote the virtue and intelligence of the people' in the community. On the other hand, the 'machinery' of government must be 'adapted to take advantage of the amount of good qualities which may at any time exist and make them instrumental to the right purposes' (Mill, 25-6). As many commentators have noted, Mill tends to emphasize the first of these criteria. What has not generally been noticed is that possession of these criteria — of these *marks* of good government — is not what *makes* the government good. What *makes* the government good is its having good effects. Virtuous citizens and appropriate governmental 'machinery' are marks of good government because they are what makes it possible for government to produce the right effects. This is quite clear from the way in which Mill introduces the idea of concentrating on the personal qualities of the citizenry. He begins by considering the problem of the administration of justice. An effective and fair judicial system requires intelligent, honest and fair-minded citizens: witnesses must be reliable, judges must refrain from taking bribes, jurors must be willing and able to consider the merits of a case dispassionately, and so on (Mill, 24). Mill uses the same example in order to explain the importance of the 'machinery' of government.

> The judicial system being given, the goodness of the administration of justice is in the compound ratio of the worth of the men composing the tribunals, and the worth of the public opinion which influences or controls them. But all the difference between a good and a bad system of judicature lies in the contrivances adopted for bringing whatever moral and intellectual worth exists in the community to bear upon the administration of justice and making it duly operative on the result (Mill, 26).

The tendency of a government to promote the virtue of its citizens, together with the quality of its 'machinery', are *criteria* of good government because governments that promote virtue and have the right machinery tend to perform the function of governments well. But the *function* of a government is to produce good decisions and good legislation — in general, to promote 'the aggregate interests of society' (Mill, 16). An ideal form of government, then, will be a government that is in harmony with itself. It will consist of institutions that affect people's character in such a way that people with that kind of character, operating those institutions, will tend to produce the best laws and decisions. To show that a form of government is desirable, one would need, in principle, to begin with an account of the goals to be achieved — an account of good legislation, for example. One would then have to demonstrate that, given the machinery of government, and given the effects of that form of government on the citizenry, we could expect good laws and policies.

Mill is a utilitarian. He holds, as noted above, that government should be so designed that it promotes 'the aggregate interests of society'. Why does he think that representative government is the form of government most likely to achieve this goal? In part, of course, the answer is that representative government is not the best form of government under *all* conditions. If, for example, citizens have acquired neither the willingness to acquiesce in *necessary* authority, nor sufficient will to take an active role in government, representative government will fail (Mill, Chapter IV). Nevertheless, Mill holds, once the requisite conditions have been satisfied, representative government is superior to any other form of government, under *any* conditions. Why?

The 'ideally best form of government', Mill says,

> is that in which the sovereignty, or supreme controlling power in the last resort, is vested in the entire aggregate of the community, every citizen not only having a voice in the exercise of that ultimate sovereignty, but being, at least occasionally, called on to take an actual part in the government by the personal discharge of some public function, local or general (Mill, 42).

This kind of government, Mill says, will both make good use of people as they are, and will tend to improve them in such a way that they will govern even better as time passes. People will be secure from bad government because they will be 'self-*protecting*' and they will be able to improve their collective lot because they will become 'self-*dependent*' (Mill, 43). In a popular form of government, the chance of injustice will be reduced because each person will stand up for his own rights. And no one stands up for a person's rights better than that person himself. Moreover, a system in which people have some control over their political situation breeds an active, vigorous citizenry. According to Mill, not only will active persons do a better job of protecting their rights, but also, active as opposed to passive persons will promote the long term interests of society.

Self government protects people against abuses, it breeds the type of citizen who will be vigilant in protecting himself, and it breeds in everyone the attitudes that a society must have in its rulers if it is to advance (Mill, 43-52).

Parts of Mill's position — the idea that democracy protects individuals against injustice by giving them a chance to stand up for their own rights, for example — are familiar to most of us.[18] But the question is whether it is really *true* that individual rights are protected in a democracy. In what kind of a democracy, operating under what kinds of voting rules, do rights get protected? Throughout most of Chapter 3, Mill seems to be thinking of a direct democracy. He concludes the chapter thus:

it is evident that the only government that can fully satisfy all the exigencies of the social state is one in which the whole people participate; that any participation, even in the smallest public function is useful; that the participation should everywhere be as great as the general degree of improvement of the community will allow; and that nothing less can be ultimately desirable than the admission of all to a share in the sovereign power of the state. But since all cannot, in a community exceeding a single small town, participate personally in any but some very minor portions of the public business, it follows that the ideal type of a perfect government must be representative (Mill, 55).

This is a non sequitur. If direct democracy is ideal, but unfeasible, it does not follow that the feasible alternative most similar, namely representative democracy, is therefore the best of the feasible alternatives. It may be the best, but we need further argument to show this. Specifically, we would need to show that it will perform functions like that of protecting the rights of individuals as well as any alternative. There are clearly difficult questions here. For example, will everyone be represented, or represented equally well, in a representative democracy? And will it make a difference whether Parliament operates on a simple majority rule or on some alternative kind of rule?

Even if we imagine that some kind of direct democracy is possible, and assume that people are vigorous in the protection of what they take to be their own rights and interests, it does not follow that each person's rights *will* be protected in a direct democracy. In Chapter V,

114

we looked at some attempts to predict the outcome of democratic decision-making processes under various assumptions about voting rules, and on the assumption that each individual would be vigorous in trying to achieve his own ends. Mill does not offer anything like this kind of analysis of democratic decision-making, but our earlier discussions should remind us that there is no guarantee that everyone will get his way. Quite the contrary. The problem of majority tyranny is still a serious problem.

As it happens, Mill does devote some later chapters (Chapter 7, especially) to the problem of designing a method of representation in which all shades of opinion achieve representation in Parliament. However, everyone's being represented in Parliament does not guarantee that everyone's rights will be respected in parliamentary decisions. After all, even direct democracy does not guarantee protection for everyone, since people may have diametrically opposed opinions as to what their rights are, and there is no reason to believe, a priori, that the person who is correct will prevail.

Mill would reply, I believe, that this objection is based on a misunderstanding of the way in which democracy works to protect people's rights. It is not because everyone has a vote that each person's rights are protected. Having a vote does not guarantee being on the winning side. The important thing about democratic government — whether direct democracy or representative democracy — is that the processes of decision-making and administration are carried out in the *open*. It is not that everyone will always have his or her way, but that whatever is done will be done in *public*. Administrators and legislators will be forced to *defend* their actions in public.

The proper function of a representative parliament, according to Mill, is not to administer, nor even to legislate, if by this we mean to write bills and enact statutes. If only because it is too large and diverse, it is ill suited to these tasks (Mill, 71-7). Its proper function is:

> to watch and control the government: to throw the light of publicity on its acts; [and] to compel a full exposition and justification of all of them which anyone considers questionable; . . . Parliament [is] at once the nation's Committee of Grievances and its Congress of Opinions — an arena in which not only the general opinion of the nation, but that of every section of it, and as far as possible of every eminent individual whom it contains, can produce itself in full light and challenge discussion; where every person in the country may

count upon finding somebody who speaks his mind, as well or better
than he could speak it himself, not to friends and partisans exclus-
ively, but in the face of opponents, to be tested by adverse controversy; where those whose opinion is overruled feel satisfied that it is
heard and set aside not by a mere act of will, but for what are
thought superior reasons . . . (Mill, 81-2).

Why think that this kind of open government, open debate of public
policy, willingness to consider grievances seriously and respond to
them, will lead to good government? Why think, for that matter, that
representatives will properly discharge their responsibility to publicize
the activities of government, to publicize criticism of the government,
and to debate the issues seriously? Won't there be a temptation, for
example, simply to ignore demands for justification when they proceed
from small minorities? There are two kinds of questions here. On the
one hand, there are questions about the likelihood that elected representatives will perform the functions expected of them according to the
theory. On the other hand, there is the question whether, even if they
do, the result will be morally good government. Mill offers, at best,
only partial answers to these questions.

In a way, each of the two questions I have raised here is a question
concerning the character of citizens. How will they respond to demands
for justification from others? What will they regard as an acceptable
justification? When will they be willing to limit their demands on others?
To what extent will they feel that they need to justify their conduct to
others? The questions I have raised above are also questions about what
morality requires. What is the relation between a policy's being acceptable to members of a community — it's being justifiable in the sense
that it is acceptable — and its being *morally* justifiable?

Now, in Mill's view, a major advantage of democracy is that it
improves the character of its citizens. On the one hand, he thinks it will
produce active, self assertive persons concerned with improving their
environment. Perhaps more important, when citizens are required 'to
exercise, for a time and in their turn, some social function', this mitigates the fact that there is little 'in most men's ordinary life to give any
largeness either to their conceptions or to their sentiments'. When a
person is required to serve on juries, or to serve in local office, '[he] is
called upon, while so engaged, to weigh interests not his own; to be
guided, in case of conflicting claims, by another rule than his private
partialities; to apply, at every turn, principles and maxims which have

116

for their reason of existence the common good' (Mill, 53-4).

As I read Mill, assumptions something like these are crucial to his theory. The open and public character of government in a representative democracy is a *desirable* feature of that kind of government only if we assume that open discussion of governmental policy tends to result in good policy choices, or at least tends to prevent bad choices. The plausibility of this assumption depends, in turn, on assumptions about the kind of policy that citizens will find acceptable. What Mill wants to claim is that the very process of open discussion leads people to adopt reasonable moral principles. It works both directly and indirectly. To the extent that citizens already have good character, public discussion of governmental policy alternatives results in good policy. To the extent that citizens lack good character, public discussion and debate tends to improve their character by leading them, for example, to appreciate the situation of others.

The question is whether any of this is true. If Mill wishes to claim that participating in government, listening to public debate of political issues, discussing these issues with acquaintances and so forth, will lead people to adopt any specific set of moral principles — utilitarian principles, for example — it is not clear how he could defend his claim. But it may be possible to provide a plausible defense of a less specific claim. Recall Rawls's conception of a 'well-ordered society' discussed in the preceding section: A well-ordered society is a society governed by commonly accepted principles of justice. Now, it does seem plausible that, when matters of public policy are subject to frequent public debate, and when most individuals are called upon, from time to time, 'to exercise some public function', that citizens will attempt to formulate principles in terms of which they will be able to defend their positions to others. Similarly, to the extent that political leaders must defend their positions publicly, they will have to formulate principles and conceptions of the common good in terms of which they can justify their positions. At least, given open institutions, and given the kind of motivational assumptions discussed in the preceding section, public functionaries will attempt to formulate coherent justifications for their policies; and these justifications will have to be capable of gaining widespread public acceptance. Such justifications will have to represent a kind of possible consensus — a possible 'fundamental charter of a well ordered society'. But principles like this satisfy at least a necessary condition for adequate moral principles. And if we assume a populace sufficiently well educated to understand the consequences of legislative

117

proposals, laws that can pass the test of public justifiability will tend to be morally justifiable laws.

5 SUMMARY, OBJECTIONS AND QUALIFICATIONS

Mill's theory of representative government, I have claimed, embodies a justification of the kind appropriate for a system of government. The argument is that representative government tends to produce morally acceptable laws and policies. At least, it tends to produce laws and policies within the bounds of the permissible as determined by reasonable moral principles. The argument needs to be filled out with a general account of moral principles; and I have attempted to provide a partial account which, when conjoined with Mill's argument, makes the argument plausible. The idea is this: Morality is a system of constraints on conduct which people could jointly acknowledge as the constraints determining the form of their association together. Thus, a good system of government is a system that leads people to formulate mutually agreeable conceptions of fundamental constraints, and it is a system that leads them to adopt laws and policies compatible with such constraints.[19] A system of representative government with an educated, responsible citizenry, and with representatives who understand their responsibility to promote serious, open discussion of governmental policy — a *public* government, we might call it — should have these consequences.

Is public government, as conceived here, feasible? This question could have different meanings. Many recent disputes about the feasibility of democratic institutions have focused on the difference between representative systems and direct democracy of one kind or another. Thus, those more or less sympathetic to current institutions have objected to advocates of greater participation — the town meeting model — that it is just impossible to operate a national government that way.[20] But clearly there is no such problem about a system of representative government. We already have one. On the other hand, existing institutions and practices are not above criticism from the perspective of the kind of theory suggested here. If there is a single idea that is central to Mill's theory, it is the idea of *open* government. In a society of any great size it is clear that the ideal of open government depends for its realization on a variety of institutions. A vigorous free press, free not only from legal limitation, but also from more subtle forms of intimida-

118

tion, is clearly essential. Open meetings laws — 'Sunshine Laws' — are also a natural step toward this ideal, as are proposals to broadcast congressional hearings and even sessions of congress. Such changes, evidently desirable in terms of this theory, are also possible.

The real problems of feasibility are not problems about the possibility of necessary institutions. They have to do with whether people — both citizens and officials of government — will comply with the spirit of open government. There is a nest of problems here. People I have claimed, naturally want to be able to justify their conduct to others. They want their own actions and their institutions to be acceptable from the perspective of mutually acceptable principles. If Mill is right, the institutions of representative government, especially when they require some citizen participation at least at some level, tend to foster the development of this natural desire. When this desire is prevalent, open government conducted in a spirit of candor and openness tends to be good government. But, the prevalence of this desire does not itself guarantee that government will be so conducted. Quite simply, well-meaning elected officials, wanting to enact justifiable policies, may lack faith in the public, and thus may decide to act undemocratically. In the short run, at least, they will not necessarily be acting wrongly. The argument for democracy, as conceived here, is an argument in terms of its long run tendencies. In the short run, it requires faith. Even in a society of well-meaning persons, democracy is not necessarily stable; it is liable to degenerate into nondemocratic alternatives.

Another kind of instability afflicts democracies. The advantage of democracy is that it *moralizes* the process of government.[21] It encourages both citizens and representatives to think of legislation and policy-making in terms of what can be justified; and it leads them to formulate principles and conceptions of the common good in terms of which they can carry out the process of justification. The result, at best, is a stable, well-ordered society, as Rawls understands this notion, with virtual unanimity on fundamental principles underwriting common laws and institutions. But another possibility is a politics built around entrenched, irreconcilable ideologies: a society divided into warring camps. What *morality* requires in a case like this cannot be specified in the abstract. Perhaps one of the ideologies is actually a reasonable morality. Perhaps neither is. In any case, there is no guarantee that the democratic process will result in reasonable laws and policies under these conditions, and it is possible that democracy itself will not long survive.[22]

A good question for empirical study is the question under what

119

conditions the 'moralizing' tendencies of democratic politics will tend to produce desirable results and under what conditions they will not. One might think that a crucial variable would be the method of voting. Specifically, one might think, a simple majority rule, either in the election of representatives or in the legislative process itself, would encourage the development of ideologies with less than universal appeal. Something closer to a unanimity rule seems more appropriate, given the emphasis on unanimity in my theory. But, as we have seen in earlier chapters, the unanimity rule is equivalent to the rule of one when that one happens to favor the status quo. Unless we assume that the status quo has some privileged status in morality, the unanimity rule is not clearly preferable to the majority rule. The ideal of democratic politics sketched here is that, whatever policies we adopt, they will have to be *justifiable* in terms of widely acceptable principles. Under majority rule, a decision *not* to change is subject to the same requirement.

Variables other than voting rules may well be even more important. The size of the community and the quality of communications, the character and educational level of citizens, and the presence or absence of castes or patterns of segregation are all likely to influence the quality of political debate and, hence, the quality of legislation. Again, it will take empirical investigation to determine just what variables affect the *moral* quality of legislation as I understand this notion here. It seems to me likely, for example, that the pressures for just legislation will be greater in a society to which people feel committed than in a society from which emigration is easy or attractive. But this conjecture requires verification.[23]

It is worth recalling, briefly, Dahl's criticism of Madison. Madison claimed, according to Dahl, that American constitutional procedures are strictly *necessary* if we are to avoid tyranny, and Dahl ridiculed that idea. I think it is also clear that no system of political institutions, by itself, is *sufficient* to prevent tyranny. I suspect Dahl would agree fully. But if there is reason to believe that democratic institutions are morally preferable to nondemocratic alternatives, they must increase the likelihood that laws and policies will conform to the requirements of an adequate morality. Whether they will do so in a particular case probably depends on factors of the kinds I have mentioned.

Many theorists have argued for democracy on the ground that it tends to protect the rights of individuals, and, in general, to produce just laws and policies. But the arguments tend to be weak. True, people have a chance to express their grievances, argue for their rights, and exercise their franchise in defense of their positions. But what we need to know is whether legitimate claims will tend to prevail and illegitimate claims to lose. Why think that? I have offered a way to strengthen the argument by suggesting assumptions about human motivation, about the dynamics of representative government, and about the nature of morality. The argument depends especially on these assumptions about morality. I have assumed that an adequate morality constitutes a kind of possible point of agreement among people concerning the limits of the permissible in their common affairs. At the beginning of this chapter, I suggested that other attempted justifications of democracy tend to assume the value of what they are trying to justify. When they assume a moral theory, for example, the moral theory is just what critics of democracy are likely to regard as in need of justification. Now, I can imagine someone objecting to the conception of morality advanced here in much the same way: The idea that what is morally right has anything to do with what people believe, or are willing to accept, or whatever, might well seem to be presupposed by a belief in democracy; and that presupposition is what bothers critics of democracy. I have some sympathy with this objection. It is probably correct, and worth noting, that unless there is *some* systematic connection between people's needs, preferences, etc., and what morality requires, then it is doubtful that democracy can be morally justified. On the other hand, we need not assume, and I do not assume here, that morality simply requires doing what the majority prefers, or that all preferences and desires need to be given equal weight, or even that they be weighted in proportion to their subjective intensity. It is more complicated than that. Moreover, I have made at least some effort to show that the conception of morality assumed here is reasonable on independent grounds.

6 COMPARISONS AND CONTRASTS

A: Participation Theory

Theories stressing the role of political participation in the democratic ideal have enjoyed a certain vogue in recent years, and some theorists of participatory democracy have appealed to the authority of John Stuart Mill. But, if I am right, participation plays a role in Mill's theory different from the role sometimes assigned to it by participation theorists. In any case, it certainly plays a different role in the theory I have sketched here and which I *claim* to find in Mill's work. Political participation, in my view, is not intrinsically good, whether we define 'politics' broadly or narrowly. It is desirable neither because it tends to stabilize government (by making people *feel* committed to political decisions), nor because the act of participation somehow gives rise to a moral obligation, on the part of citizens, to comply with political decisions. I argued in Chapter III that participation does not have the latter effect, and whether or not it has the former, that effect is not necessarily desirable. Whether it is depends on the moral acceptability of the government's substantive policies.

In his critique of revisionist theory, Jack Walker said 'public policy should result from extensive, informed discussion and debate'.[24] In my view, and I believe in Mill's, a system of government is to be evaluated in terms of its legislative and policy decisions. Nevertheless, the conception of democracy defended in this chapter is like Walker's in its emphasis on open government, though I go beyond anything Walker says by offering a defense of this conception of democracy grounded in moral theory.

The idea of open and public debate can be distinguished from the idea of a participatory society as described in the work of Bachrach or Pateman, but this latter idea can also be given a defense in the context of the theory developed here. The defense parallels the elaboration of participation theory adumbrated at the conclusion of Chapter III. To the extent that popular participation in government is desirable, it is desirable because it contributes either directly or indirectly to the quality of government. However, in a representative democracy, the quality of government depends to a large extent on the character of citizens, since the policies adopted tend to be those that can be justified in public debate. Thus, if experience in the exercise of public functions, in group decision-making, and the like, leads people to take an interest in the general acceptability of their actions and decisions, and if it leads them to adopt reasonable moral principles, then participation of these kinds contributes to the quality of democratic government. Mill speculates that participation has consequences like these, and so regards such participation as a desirable aspect of a system of representative government. This is not implausible, but neither is it obvious. It requires the kind of empirical confirmation discussed in Pateman's *Participation and Democratic Theory*.[25] Specifically, it is worth asking what kind of principles people will come to accept as a result of participatory decision-making in their work or in local affairs. When they turn from local to national issues, what attitudes will they bring with them? Will the experience of participatory decision-making in local or professional affairs leave them with a desire to seek policies acceptable to ever widening circles of people, or will it leave them with a firm commitment to ideologies favoring narrow local, class or professional interests?

B: Procedural Fairness

A direct appeal to the idea of fair procedures plays no role in the argument for democratic government sketched here. Consequently, it is not *necessarily* an objection to a specific system of representative government that it is unfair or unequal in some respect. Nevertheless, some features of systems of government that could be defended in terms of a demand for fairness can also be defended in terms of my theory. I noted in Chapter II that the idea of fairness seems to yield an argument for simple majority rule as opposed to unanimity or 2/3 majority rules. But, if we want a system in which all policies and institutions must be justifiable in terms of generally acceptable principles, then we have another argument in favor of simple majority rule. Since simple majority rule does not give any preference to existing institutions over new proposals, it subjects all institutions to the test of justifiability. Again, while there is no *direct* argument for equal (or proportional) representation of all classes, or interests, or geographical entities, there is an argument against policies that systematically prevent certain groups from making their concerns known. We need to encourage the development of principles acceptable to *everyone*, and of legislation justifiable in terms of those principles.

One qualification is in order. The conception of morality I have suggested in this chapter is that a morality is a system of constraints on conduct acceptable to everyone. This conception of morality makes it seem at least plausible that institutions of representative democracy will result in *morally* acceptable substantive laws and policies. But, as noted in Chapter II, it is *conceivable* that agreement on constraints will include, but be limited to, an agreement on fair procedures for assessing institutions or rules of conduct. In that case, there would be a direct argument for fair procedures.

C: Autonomy and Popular Sovereignty

How does the position outlined in this chapter differ from the theory of democracy as popular sovereignty — the theory that democracy secures individual autonomy because citizens in a democracy are self governing? The idea behind the latter theory seems to be this: We take people as they are, each person having a certain system of preferences over possible social arrangements. If people are in complete agreement, there is no problem. Democratic government legislates according to their (unanimous) will. However, we cannot expect this kind of unanimity in general. Hence, the idea of self government requires that we develop an account of *the will of the people*. Such an account defines the will of the people as some function of individual preferences, no matter what they happen to be. A democratic form of government is simply a form of government designed to legislate in accordance with the will of the people, as defined.

What this kind of theory requires, I argued in Chapter IV, is a conception of the will of the people satisfying a number of conditions of various types. Arrow's theorem suggests that we will not find any such conception, since he shows that no rule amalgamating individual preferences into a social preference can satisfy what he regards as minimal conditions. But, even if we allow ourselves to weaken or alter some of his conditions, the resulting account will not lead to a theory of democracy as self government that gives rise to a justification of democracy. It is hard to see why self government, defined in terms of the kind of conception of the people's will in question, is desirable.

I argue in this chapter that government ought to accord with the unanimous will of the people, when this unanimity consists of agreement on principles constituting the basis of a stable, well-ordered society. Of course, we will ordinarily not have this kind of unanimity, but one aim of government, as conceived here, is to try to create it. And when there is a lack of agreement, governmental policy should accord with principles that *could* be generally accepted. Policy should be justifiable in terms of a possible consensus. Democratic government, ideally, prevents the adoption of policies that cannot be justified to most people; and the process of open discussion and debate leads individuals to adopt standards which, in turn, can gain wider and wider acceptance. The long-run result should be consensus on principles, and laws and policies consistent with those principles.

D: Economic Theories

Economics tells us that even people with largely conflicting aims and purposes can often strike mutually beneficial bargains. Economic theories of democracy treat a political system, on analogy with the market, as a set of institutions mediating the process of bargaining and exchange.

It amalgamates individual choices and produces a social decision. Economists interested in *describing* political institutions ask the same questions that they ask when studying different economic institutions: Do these institutions favor certain preferences over others? How do they respond to changes in tastes or preferences? Do they lead to optimal patterns of preference satisfaction? Theorists concerned with the *evaluation* of democratic institutions tend to argue for them on the ground that they do result in such optimal levels of satisfaction and thus that they embody an analog of consumer sovereignty.

Like theories based on popular sovereignty, economic theories take preferences as given, though these theories do not claim that democracy guarantees self government or autonomy in any strong sense. With some plausibility, economic theorists can claim that democratic institutions result in a kind of optimal preference satisfaction. But the precise pattern of satisfaction — whose preferences will be satisfied to what degree — will depend on the precise structure of the bargaining problem facing citizens. The pattern of satisfaction will depend in part on factors like the intensity of different desires, but it will also depend on a variety of other factors.

The theory I defend in this chapter is similar to an economic theory in its abstract, quasi-deductive character. I begin with a general idea about the nature of democratic politics, an abstract account of morality, and an assumption about the motives of typical people. What I then argue is that democracy will result, given these assumptions, in a set of laws and policies consistent with the requirements of an adequate morality. Prima facie, there are two basic differences between my theory and the kind of economic theory discussed in Chapter V. First, by stressing the role of public debate and open justification, I argue for a different conception of the actual operation of democratic governments. I suggest that certain factors overlooked in economic theories have a significant impact on the actual outcome of democratic decision-making. Second, I offer a different account of the standards by which governmental decisions are to be judged.

One question about my own theory, from the perspective of economic theories, is whether I (and other writers like Mill) are right about the efficacy of factors like open and public debate. Will representative government in fact tend to produce something more like the kind of bargain or compromise among interest groups suggested by economic theories? How important this question is will depend on the answer to another question, namely, to what extent do the requirements of an adequate morality, as I have defined this notion, diverge from the requirements of Pareto efficiency? If an adequate morality requires nothing more than Pareto optimality, then, even if the economic theorists' conception of the dynamics of democratic politics is correct, democracy will still be justified on my view. Now, this question seems especially pressing since, on my view, an adequate morality is (in part) a system of constraints defining a possible society-wide consensus. But the economic theorists have suggested that the only standard unanimously acceptable is the standard of Pareto optimality.

It is worth noting these points because it reminds us that the critique of economic theories, like, for example, the critique of the theory based on the idea of fair procedures, depends ultimately on the substantive content of an adequate moral theory. However, the idea that the Pareto criterion does not exhaust the content of an adequate social morality is not implausible on the conception of morality defended here. An adequate morality is not just any consensus. It is a consensus on certain overriding constraints that can be publicly avowed by free and independent persons, and that will be stable over time. My assumption is that these further conditions put some limits on the range of possible, adequate moralities.

Any morality, including one based on some version of the Pareto principle, will require or permit that some gain at the expense of others – that some desires be frustrated and others satisfied. Any morality will require that people refrain, on occasion, from even attempting to satisfy their desires in certain ways. Sooner or later sacrifices will be required of most everyone. The question is what constraints, based on what considerations, people will be willing to accept over time. Any set of principles, I suggest, incorporates, in effect, a *proposal* that certain interests, desires, or preferences are to be regarded as more important than others.[26] Thus, it may propose, as Rawls's principles of justice do, that desires for a certain share of 'primary goods' (rights and opportunities, income and wealth) be given priority. Such principles will constitute an adequate morality to the extent that people already give priority to these goods in their own calculations, or will be willing to adopt this scheme of priorities on reflection, in the interest of having a commonly acceptable standard of justification. Given agreement on the central importance of some such goods in each person's life, it is not implausible that there could be consensus on principles requiring, say, an equal distribution of those goods. What I doubt is that people would agree, under any circumstances, to principles making one's right to a

126

certain benefit any simple function of the intensity of one's subjective preference for that benefit or of one's 'bargaining position' in the market distributing that benefit. According to the economic analysis of democratic institutions, such factors will tend to determine the allocation of benefits. Hence, the economic analysis of democracy fails to provide us in any direct way with a justification of democracy.

E: Pluralism in Political Sociology

Much of the modern work on democratic theory is the work of political sociologists. It is this work against which the theorists of participatory democracy reacted. The main aim of this sociological work, evidently, is to describe the operation of modern, democratic systems of government. Society is seen as a collection of interest groups and coalitions of interest groups striving to attain their several goals within the constraints of political institutions. The democratic political system provides interest groups with channels through which they can attempt to achieve their political goals. But, while these channels are open to most everyone, success is guaranteed to no group. Instead, any one group's ability to achieve its political goals is determined by the extent to which other groups have contrary goals, by the relative political power of these groups, by their willingness to compromise and so forth.

Given this general picture of society and of democratic politics, there seem to be a number of interesting problems for empirical study. Some theorists study the effects on this process of different institutional forms, strong presidential systems, and parliamentary systems with or without proportional representation, for example.[27] Other theorists have studied the effects of various social, economic, demographic and psychological factors on the development of interest groups and on the distribution of their membership. Theorists then combine the results of investigations like these and attempt to specify the conditions under which democratic systems will manage to retain the loyalty of citizens and remain stable over time without ceasing to be democratic. In general, it seems to be held, there is a range of possible democratic systems, and a range of possible configurations of classes or interest groups such that, given any of those systems and any of those configurations of interests, there is a good chance of stable democratic government.[28] Conflicting interest groups, though seldom able to gain everything they want through the political process, nevertheless remain loyal if only because they doubt that they can do better in any other system.

The sociological theorists under discussion here are notable for their apparent lack of interest in questions of justification or evaluation. To be sure, it is quite clear that they want to avoid authoritarian systems, either of the left or of the right. But, given this dominant concern, they seem to be mainly interested in specifying the prerequisites for stability in democratic systems. We attempt to extract a justification of democracy from their work only at our peril. But I suspect they would argue for democracy, if forced to do so, in roughly the way in which the economic theorists might: democracy makes it possible for the diverse groups in a pluralistic society to achieve their sometimes conflicting goals to the greatest extent possible.

The function of a just political system, I have argued, is to produce laws and policies consistent with the requirements of an adequate morality. A just political system will tend to satisfy those interests whose satisfaction is required by morality, and it will tend to ignore those interests whose satisfaction is inconsistent with morality. But there is nothing in the conception of democratic pluralism discussed here to lead us to expect these results. To the extent that governmental policy is determined *simply* by chance configurations of interest groups, by which groups make the most noise or have the most clout, or by chance quirks of a particular system of voting or representation, there is a clear danger of injustice. But even when policy represents something like a compromise or bargain among conflicting groups, there is no reason to believe that it is just. Hence, I reject the (implicit or explicit) justification of democracy found in either the economic or sociological theories of democracy. But to do this is not to reject the institutions they seek to justify, nor is it to deny that they are democratic institutions. In an open system of representative government, I have suggested, policies tend to be rejected when they cannot be justified publicly. Moreover, the process of open and public discussion leads to the development of conceptions of justice and the public good that have the capacity to be widely accepted. Hence, policy proposals tend to be rejected when they are inconsistent with such conceptions.

What I offer here is an *hypothesis* about the operation of constitutional democracy. If it is right, however, there is an important check on the influence of (some) interest groups. Groups that cannot find a way to justify their demands in terms of generally acceptable principles will tend to be ignored. Political parties that cannot find a way, consistent with their professed principles, to appeal to certain groups, will not appeal to them. Political parties do not simply assemble a platform that will appeal to groups representing any 51 per cent of the electorate.

They seek a platform that they are willing to defend before the whole electorate. The tendency, again, is to subject political activity to moral constraints. But not only does this tend to preclude political recognition of certain interests; it may well also, in the long run, lead people to alter their own conceptions of their interests. The long-run equilibrium is, in Rawls's phrase, 'a well-ordered society'.

I have said that this is an hypothesis. If it is a correct hypothesis, then there is an argument in favor of (roughly) the institutions of modern constitutional democracy that has been overlooked. But there is a great deal of room for empirical investigation. First, does this hypothesis explain anything? How well can we explain legislation and governmental policy without making reference to the kind of appeal to principle and demand for justification described here? Second, what kind of democratic system (parliamentary, multi-party, two-party, etc.) does most to encourage this aspect of democratic politics? Third, what social and psychological conditions must obtain if democracy is to work as it should?

CONCLUSIONS

This chapter is far too long to summarize. My central aim has been to argue for the political institution of modern constitutional democracies on the ground that they tend to produce just government, or, at least, to prevent serious injustice. An argument like this presupposes some kind of account of what justice requires. The requirements of justice are among the requirements of morality, and a morality, I suggest, is a set of principles capable of serving as the public charter of a well-ordered society of free and independent persons. It is a basis for consensus on the evaluation of shared institutions and practices. What makes democracy desirable is that it is a system of *open* government in which those who govern are called upon, from time to time, to account for their actions, to justify and defend them, in public. Open debate, in turn, fosters the development of a public morality. General acceptance of such a morality, in a democracy, precludes legislation and policies contrary to the morality.

Problems remain. First, at a number of points in this chapter I have indicated the need for empirical investigation. The basic question is just whether (or, better, under what conditions) democratic government will work as I have suggested it might work ideally. Second, even if it does work as I suggest, does this make it legitimate? Again and again, I have argued that this question is ambiguous. The argument here is that democracy is a desirable form of government, in the sense that it is a good solution to the problem of constitutional design. Under favorable conditions, at least, I would recommend the adoption of a democratic constitution to people establishing a government.

Suppose conditions are favorable, suppose we have a democratic constitution, and suppose it is generally respected. Should we obey the law? Must we obey the law? May we obey the law? Always? Sometimes? Never? If these are the questions one has in mind when inquiring about the legitimacy of democratic government, I have not yet attempted an answer. I shall turn to these questions next.

VII

LAW AND MORALITY: THE PROBLEM OF POLITICAL OBLIGATION

We need not understand the question whether democracy is a good form of government as the question whether the laws in a democracy are always morally binding on citizens. Whether citizens in a democracy are morally required, or even permitted, to obey all of its laws is one question; whether democracy is a good solution to the problem of constitutional design is another. That we need to distinguish these two questions has been one of my main themes throughout the preceding chapters, and I have focused on the second question. In this chapter I shall turn to the first question, the traditional question of political obligation.

I have argued in favor of a representative form of government, conducting its business in the open, with firm guarantees of free speech and free press. I have argued for this kind of government on the ground that it will tend to produce laws and policies consistent with the requirements of morality. If I am right, however, this is only a tendency. Under the best conditions, there is no guarantee that all laws will be consistent with morality. And some laws that are consistent with morality may not correspond to moral requirements: the actions enjoined by such laws may be morally permissible but not morally required. For these two reasons, it is not obvious that citizens in a democracy are morally required to obey all the laws of their government. In *one* respect, democracy has not been shown to be legitimate.

What I have said here may seem strange. It may seem strange that we should not be morally required to comply with the decisions of a procedure that is justifiable from a moral point of view. After all, it might seem, insofar as statutes, or articles of a bill of rights, are based on moral

131

considerations — constitute implementations of moral principles — we clearly have a moral obligation to comply with those statues or articles. So, the case of democratic decision-making processes seems to be anomalous. It is based on moral considerations, but we are not always required to obey it. I shall argue here, however, that this case is not anomalous. The problems connected with the obligation to comply with the decisions of a morally justified decision procedure are like problems concerning the question why we ought to comply with the requirements of a morally justified statute or article of a bill of rights. The problem, in general, is this: a morally justified statute, based on a moral principle, may sometimes require conduct not required by the moral principle on which it is based. Conduct that violates a morally justified statute, even when that statute is based on moral considerations, may not conflict with those moral considerations themselves. Even in the (apparently) most straightforward kind of case, then, either there may be situations in which there is no moral obligation to comply with a morally justifiable law, or we must find an explanation for that obligation in considerations other than the considerations that justify the law in the first place. If there are such other considerations, however, we must ask whether they generate an obligation to comply with the outcome of a morally justified decision-making process even in those cases in which it errs.

In the first section of what follows I shall explain further and attempt to defend the position I have outlined here concerning the relation between law and morality. In succeeding sections, I shall consider possible responses to what I say in Section 1. The responses I consider will fall far short of exhausting all the possibilities, but discussing them should contribute substantially to an understanding of the problems of political obligation. In particular, the possibilities I discuss are all relevant to the question whether there is a general obligation to comply with the law in a constitutional democracy.

1 LAW AND MORALITY

When a law or system of laws is morally justifiable in terms of a reasonable morality, what is the relation between the justifiable laws and the moral principles in terms of which they are justified? I asked this question in Chapter VI in connection with the specific question what conditions a political decision-making procedure must satisfy in order to be morally justifiable. The answer, I said, depends on substantive moral theory; but, I suggested, a reasonable morality would demand of a legislative procedure primarily that it be as likely as possible to produce laws and policies protecting substantive moral rights and promoting the substantive goals of morality. A political decision procedure is morally justifiable to the extent that it tends to produce justifiable laws and decisions. But when is a law morally justifiable? A partial answer, analogous to the above, is this: a law is morally justified if it is an essential part of a system of laws which, as well as any alternative system of laws, protects moral rights and promotes compliance with moral principles. This is only a *partial* answer because it offers only a sufficient condition for a law's being justifiable. There may be laws that are permissible but play no essential role in protecting moral rights or in promoting morally required benefits. Such laws might still be desirable given the interests of a particular community. I speak of *systems* of laws because it seems likely that more than one set of laws might be functionally equivalent; and I speak of a law's playing an essential role in such a system to exclude those laws which could be subtracted from a system without diminishing its efficacy.

If we imagine a system of laws satisfying the above conditions, what will particular laws look like? To what extent will they correspond to specific moral rules or principles? How we answer this question will, of course, depend on our views about morality as well as our views about the likely effects of different kinds of laws and policies. A morality, I assume, will include a variety of elements. It may have a structure like this: at the most general level, it will contain a specification of kinds of human harm and benefit relevant to the rightness or wrongness of acts, and it will also contain some kind of ranking of the relative importance of these harms and benefits. Thus, a morality may specify that certain forms of bodily harm or deprivation of physically needed goods along with deprivation of freedom or opportunity are harms, and it may specify that health, human affection, and certain kinds of freedom or autonomy are desirable. Given such a list, a morality should also include an account of what people are required to do by way of preventing harms and promoting benefits. Such principles of conduct will not necessarily be derivable from a list of harms and benefits in any obvious way. Preventing harms of one kind may involve producing harms of another kind. Hence, implicit in a set of principles of conduct will be some weighting of the relative importance of harms and benefits. A morality could also give expression to underlying beliefs about legitimate interests and their relative importance by assigning people rights to certain things and by interpreting these rights by specifying what they permit and require. Some rights, like principles of conduct, will have direct implications for what people can do to one another independent of institutional structures. Other rights will be conditional in that they will specify the form that institutional structures must take if they are to be morally acceptable. If we look at morality in this way, the important thing to note is that rights and principles of conduct depend ultimately for their rationale on a conception of human good and harm. A set of principles and a system of rights is acceptable to the extent that it results in, and apportions reasonably, basic human goods (together with the avoidance of harms).

On the assumption that laws are justifiable if, taken together, they serve to protect moral rights and promote compliance with moral principles, there remains a question about the extent to which particular justifiable laws will resemble the rules and principles on which they are based. How, specifically, would one argue for a law or a constitutional right, if one were thinking of justification in this way? What sort of considerations would be relevant? Consider, to begin with, constitutional provisions conferring powers on officials or denying such powers. One important question in the case of such powers is whether they are likely to be misused, either intentionally or unintentionally. A plausible, if partial, argument for a constitutional right to privacy — a prohibition on 'unreasonable searches and seizures' — is that an unlimited power to search can be easily abused. In these times, it is not hard to imagine an administration in power using information gathered from FBI wiretaps for political blackmail or leaking the information to the press at strategic times to embarrass political opponents and other critics.[1] There are similar arguments, of course, in support of guarantees of free speech and free press. Only here, perhaps more clearly than in the former case, the problem of unintentional abuse is as great or greater than the problem of intentional abuse. Not only can an administration knowingly use censorship merely for its own aggrandisement, but it can also censor important truths out of ignorance, but for perfectly laudable motives.

In each of these cases, the argument for a certain constitutional immunity — for a limit on the power of the government to act in certain ways — is based largely on the need to maintain the integrity of the political process. But this is still a *moral* argument for such limits if we assume that the relevant features of the political process contribute to the likelihood that it will result in morally desirable legislation. These rules contribute, at least indirectly, to the protection of moral rights and legitimate moral interests. Presumably, many of the rules governing procedures in criminal trials can also be justified, at least partly, in this way. These rules insure the integrity of procedures which, in turn, tend to protect moral rights and secure compliance with moral principles. What we need to note about the arguments so far considered is that, while they are relevant to the moral justification of the laws in question, they make no *direct* reference to any moral principle. The conduct prohibited is prohibited not on the ground that it is itself morally wrong but on the ground that, if permitted, it might increase the probability of (other) moral wrongs, or because it *could* be wrong when *some* people engage in it, under *some* circumstances.

The kind of argument I have just described does not apply only to laws governing the behavior of public officials. Laws against homicide are clearly to be justified, primarily, by direct reference to moral rules prohibiting killing. But consider the case of euthanasia. Philippa Foot has recently argued[2] that there may be some cases in which 'non-voluntary, passive euthanasia' is justified. That is, there may be cases in which it would be justifiable to withdraw or withhold artificial means of preserving life when the patient is unable to give his consent (because he is an infant, or is comatose, for example). In her view, however, this would be justifiable only if it was done for the benefit of the patient, or at least could not be said to harm the patient. This suggests the possibility of a law permitting infanticide in cases of serious birth defects, perhaps granting parents the power to decide when the option should be exercised. Foot argues, however, given contemporary attitudes, that such legislation would be a mistake.[3] While there are cases in which infanticide might genuinely be a benefit for an infant, and might thus be permissible, parents might sometimes seek the death of their defective children not for the child's sake, but for their own sake. The danger of abuse counsels rejection of a more liberal law.[4]

Both in the case of certain constitutional limitations on governmental authority and in the case of laws governing homicide, I have suggested a moral justification for a law which prohibits some morally permissible conduct. The idea is that we evaluate a law in terms of its tendency to promote, in practice, the goals set by morality. We must ask ourselves not just what morality actually requires, but also how the law will be interpreted, applied and enforced by ordinary, fallible and corrupt human beings. This test is likely to result in a divergence between the

135

requirements of morality and the requirements of law. Now, the kind of practical consideration and probabilistic calculations that go into the justification of laws are also relevant to the justification of legislative procedures. The latter case is not anomalous. In each case, the reason for divergence between moral requirements and the requirements of justifiable institutions is similar. Whatever problems there are about explaining the obligation to comply in one case are also present in the other.

Clearly, the view I am advancing here can be criticized in a number of ways. In arguing that laws can be morally justified although they do not correspond to independent moral principles I am making assumptions of three kinds: (1) assumptions about the type of argument that is adequate to justify a law, (2) assumptions about the character and ability of typical citizens and public officials, and (3) assumptions about the scope and content of moral principles. To the extent that one or another of these assumptions is mistaken, my argument may be mistaken. Consider again the case of constitutional limits on censorship and on invasions of privacy. My argument for these was, broadly speaking, consequentialist. I argued for freedom of expression, for example, on the ground that the power to regulate expression might be, intentionally or unintentionally, misused or used to bad purpose. But here, and in the case of rights to privacy, it can plausibly be argued that these rights are much more directly supported by moral principles. Censorship, or eavesdropping, at least under certain circumstances or for certain reasons, may be morally wrong in itself. Even if these constitutional restrictions can be defended indirectly, we cannot conclude that there is no moral requirement to comply with them unless we at least consider the possibility of moral principles that would support them more directly. Whether there are such principles, I suggested earlier, will depend on the kinds of human harm and benefit that underlie morality and provide the rationale for its requirements.[5] Still, the case of euthanasia and laws prohibiting it suggests that, even when a law is supported directly by a moral principle, we might best secure compliance with that principle by a law extending more widely than the moral principle itself. (T. M. Scanlon has argued[6] in favor of a principle of freedom of expression which, in effect, prohibits censorship for certain reasons, but would permit it in some cases which might now be proscribed by the first amendment. It does not follow, however, that the first amendment should be changed or interpreted as less of a blanket prohibition of censorship. If the line between morally permissible and impermissible censorship is hard to draw in practice, a blanket legal prohibition might be best. This will depend, however, on calculations of the long term effects of such a prohibition. Are there cases, for example, in which the power to censor might be very important from a moral point of view?)

I began this chapter with the question whether, if democracy is justified only in the way I have suggested, we are left with the consequence that democracy is illegitimate in the sense that citizens are not morally required to comply with its laws. The problem is that democracy will sometimes produce morally unjustifiable laws, and so, it would seem, the requirement that we comply with moral principles will not necessarily lead to the requirement that we comply with the law in a democracy. But, if we think of the obligation to comply with justifiable laws or institutional forms as just an instance of the requirement that we comply with independent moral principles, the problem of political obligation stems from sources deeper than the occasional imperfections of legislative procedures. Given certain reasonable assumptions, I claimed that many morally justified laws will require conduct not required by the moral principles on which they are based. Hence, there may be many cases in which the requirement that we comply with moral principles may not require that we comply with morally justified laws. (As a corollary, of course, even if a democracy produced nothing but morally justifiable laws, there would be a problem about the obligation to comply with those laws.) Now, unless there is something radically wrong with the argument so far, it seems to me that there is good theoretical reason, quite apart from the theory of democracy, to stress the distinction between the justification of laws and institutional forms on the one hand and the question of the obligation to comply with their directives on the other.

What I have done so far is simply set the stage. It certainly does not follow from what I have said here that there is no moral obligation to comply with the law in the various problematic cases discussed. The idea that there is no such obligation is one possible response to what I have said, and I shall discuss that response in the next section. In subsequent sections I shall discuss other responses: first, the response that I am wrong about the nature of law and legal requirements or about the nature of reasonable moral principles; and, second, the response that the obligation to obey morally justified laws — and perhaps *any* law resulting from justifiable constitutional procedures — is to be explained by reference to certain special principles of political obligation.

2 AN ACT UTILITARIAN VIEW

One possible response to what I have said about the relation between justifiable laws and moral principles is to agree with it and then conclude that there is sometimes no moral obligation to comply with justifiable laws in cases in which the requirements of the law diverge from the requirements of morality. For reasons which will emerge as we proceed, this is a natural response for a utilitarian, and it has been advocated forcefully by Rolf Sartorius in his recent book *Individual Conduct and Social Norms.*[7] Sartorius accepts Act Utilitarianism (AU) as a principle of morally right conduct. AU states, roughly, that whenever one is faced with a choice, one ought to do that act which will produce at least as much happiness (utility) as any alternative act. However, Sartorius also grants a number of standard objections to utilitarianism,[8] one of which is the objection that people acting on AU will fail to produce as much utility as they would if they were to act on some alternative principle. Various reasons are given for this claim. One reason is that people acting on AU, in the sense that they more or less conscientiously try to do so, will often make mistaken calculations. Another, more interesting, reason is that persons can correctly apply AU but, paradoxically, promote less utility than they would have if, in concert, they had acted otherwise. In these cases, analogs of the prisoners' dilemma, production of some good requires large scale, but not necessarily universal cooperation among the members of a group.[9] A water shortage may provide an example. Unless most people curtail their use of water, there will be a disaster. But each may reason, correctly, that he has no influence over the others, that it will do no good to conserve if he acts alone, and that the others will reason similarly. Hence, none cooperates, and there is a disaster. Alternatively, if *everyone* is cooperating, a given act utilitarian may well reason, correctly, that his cooperation is unnecessary and that he should not cooperate. In general, it seems, act utilitarians will not necessarily initiate cooperation when they should, and, even if cooperation does get under way, they may not do their part.

Utilitarians have responded to this kind of problem in a variety of ways, including rejection of AU as a principle of morally right conduct for individuals. Sartorius retains AU as an account of morally right conduct for individuals, but argues that laws and other social rules and conventions should be so designed that they lead people to act in ways that tend to maximize utility even when this involves laws requiring people to act contrary to the principle of act utilitarianism. Thus, if people are likely in certain cases to misapply AU, and if a certain type of act is almost always the right act in those cases, there ought to be a law requiring that type of act across the board. (This corresponds, of course, to the kind of case I have discussed above in which I emphasized the importance of avoiding intentional or unintentional abuse.) Similarly, if some kind of cooperation is necessary for some great benefit, it may be justifiable to require this cooperation by law even though, once the law secures general cooperation, it will sometimes be permissible on utilitarian grounds for an individual to disobey this law.

In defending this position, Sartorius realizes, he is led to reject what he calls the 'reflection principle'.[10] According to the reflection principle, if it is morally correct for an individual to do something, then any law, judicial decision, or social rule must permit his doing that thing and must not prohibit it or penalize it. Sartorius can consistently reject the reflection principle while retaining his act utilitarianism. The key point is that the situation facing an act utilitarian legislator is different from the situation facing an agent deciding what to do in a particular situation. A legislator is in a position to determine, at one stroke, what a great number of individuals will do. An individual acting in his private capacity generally does not have this kind of power. What AU requires a legislator to enjoin when he is making a law may be different from what it would require him to do, or to advise another individual to do, in a particular case. (Consider, again, the water rationing case.)

The principle Sartorius rejects, the reflection principle, is *like* the principle I implicitly rejected when I said above that a morally justified law may require (or prohibit) conduct not required (or prohibited) by the moral principles on which the law is based. There is a difference though. In rejecting the reflection principle, Sartorius says there are cases in which it is right, *all things considered*, to do some act x while it is also right that there is a law against doing x. All I have said so far is that there are cases in which it is right that there is a law against x, even though, *in terms of the moral principles on which the law is based*, it is right to do x. This is an important difference since I have left open the possibility that there might be overriding moral reasons for obeying the law independent of the principles on which the law is based. Since Sartorius accepts only one moral principle, AU, the possibility I have just mentioned is not open to him. If the law is a good law, the decision to enact it is based on AU; but, if the law requires acts not required by AU, there is no other moral principle that might require those acts. The acts are not morally required, and so there are cases in which there is no moral obligation to comply with a morally justified law.

The situation here is rather complex, since the very existence of a law, whether or not it is based correctly on utilitarian considerations, can alter the outcome of a utilitarian's calculation to favor obedience. If nothing else, the likelihood of unhappiness resulting from punishment will argue in favor of obedience for a proponent of AU. Still, there can be situations in which a utilitarian can correctly decide that he should not obey the law, even when, in terms of his own principles, the law is justified.

In terms of his act utilitarian moral theory, Sartorius offers an especially clear account of how one can accept a moral theory and justify, by reference to that moral theory, laws that do not coincide with its requirements. As Sartorius sees it, what holds at the level of specific statutes also holds at the level of constitutional design when one is writing a bill of rights or designing legislative or judicial procedures. In all of these cases, the requirements of justifiable rules or the results of justifiable procedures may fail to coincide with the requirements of morality. Sartorius concludes that there is no general moral obligation, even an overridable 'prima facie obligation', to comply with the law. But now we must ask to what extent these conclusions depend on the assumption that act utilitarianism is the correct moral theory. There are two claims to be discussed: (1) the claim that the requirements of good laws may not coincide with the requirements of the principles on which they are based and (2) the response to this first claim that, therefore, there is sometimes no obligation to comply with the law when law and morality diverge. Sartorius defends the first claim from the perspective of an act utilitarian, but I argued for it in the first section of this chapter without assuming any particular moral theory. Given the first claim, and assuming act utilitarianism, the second claim seems to follow automatically. If the requirements of the law diverge from the requirements of AU, there are no further principles within AU by reference to which we could derive an obligation to comply with the law in cases of divergence. However, in a morality with a variety of independent principles, even if the first claim were correct, the second would not necessarily follow. In the next section I shall examine in more detail the question whether the first claim is plausible even if we do not accept AU. In the fourth section I shall consider possible moral principles from which we could derive a general obligation to obey the law even if we accepted the first claim.

3 THE CONTENT OF MORALITY AND THE INTERPRETATION OF LAW

The question here is whether the valid laws of a morally justifiable legal system will require or prohibit conduct not required or prohibited by the moral principles in terms of which the laws are justified in the first place. I have said that the answer is 'yes', but this answer might plausibly be criticized in two ways. On the one hand, it could be argued that the principles of a reasonable morality will resemble the laws of a good legal system much more than the principle of utility, say, will resemble the laws of a system justifiable on utilitarian grounds. On the other hand, it might be argued that a sensible account of a justifiable legal system — in particular, a sensible account of how laws should be applied and interpreted — will have the consequence that law and morality tend to coincide. In many cases of apparent divergence between the requirements of a statute and the requirements of morality there is not a real divergence. *Properly interpreted and applied*, the statute will not diverge from morality so sharply.

1 Let me begin with the second of these two suggestions. Given a statute or an article of a bill of rights designed to protect some moral right or bring about compliance with some moral principle, how is that statute or article to be interpreted? What, exactly, does it require, and to what extent might moral considerations — like the considerations on which the law is based — be relevant to its interpretation? This is a disputed question in jurisprudence. It is essentially connected to questions about the definition of law and about the nature and proper limits of 'judicial discretion'.[11]

A significant component in a reasonable moral argument for a constitutional protection of free expression, I suggested above, is the claim that censorship, if permitted, would be likely to be misapplied, either intentionally or unintentionally. This kind of argument — it has been called an argument 'not against censorship but against mistaken censors'[12] — is, of course, the kind of argument a utilitarian might offer for many kinds of constitutional right.[13] This kind of utilitarian argument for having a blanket prohibition against censorship is equally an argument for a strict interpretation and application of the prohibition. This assumes that there are few, if any, cases in which censorship would be of great value. But, if there are few such cases, if we have the same doubts about the integrity and competence of judges that we have concerning censors, and if weakening the prohibition through precedent setting decisions would weaken its deterrent force, then a utilitarian could reasonably argue for a strict interpretation. But what about cases in which the strict meaning of the constitution is genuinely open to doubt? May a utilitarian here conclude that judges should decide cases by a direct application of the utilitarian principle? If we answer 'yes', then the range of cases in which the requirements of law and the requirements of morality diverge – assuming utilitarianism – will not be as great as it might be. A utilitarian can argue, however, that there are good utilitarian reasons for judges to appeal not directly to utility, but to what the law requires – even when what the law requires is in doubt. This, I say, is a *possible* position for a utilitarian, but it is difficult to work out in detail. It requires that one spell out what one means by 'the requirements of the law' in those areas in which it is those requirements that appear to be vague to the point of indeterminacy. More specifically, it demands that the requirements of law not be defined simply by reference to something like the positive morality underlying the law.

In a series of important papers, beginning with 'The Model of Rules',[14] Ronald Dworkin has argued against the view that judges, faced with hard decisions where the law seems unclear for one reason or another, come to have discretionary authority and rightfully become legislators. Even in cases not covered (or not covered unambiguously) by explicit statutes or other written laws, the job of the judge is still to decide what the law requires and apply it. However, Dworkin comes close to saying that the *moral* views underlying the written law are *themselves* the main determinant of what the *law* requires in areas where the written law is vague. This would amount to saying, in the case of the utilitarian legal system discussed in the preceding paragraph, that judges should appeal directly to the principle of utility in cases of vagueness or uncertainty. Moreover, in a legal system based on a nonutilitarian morality with a plurality of principles, the result of adopting Dworkin's conception of interpretation would seem to be a very close coincidence between the requirements of law and the requirements of morality. Consider the case of constitutional protections of freedom of expression. If we suppose there is a distinct moral principle protecting this freedom, at least in certain situations or for certain purposes, then, to begin with, the explicit requirements of a justifiable law might coincide much more nearly to those of morality than they would if the law were supported solely by the principle of utility. In addition, to the extent that we adopt Dworkin's view, areas of vagueness in the law will be filled out by direct appeal to underlying moral principles.

The main question, recall, is this: in a morally justifiable legal system, will there often be cases in which the law requires (or prohibits) conduct not required (or prohibited) by moral principles on which the law is based? What I have argued in this section is that the answer to this question depends in part on the extent to which, in a good legal system, judges and others empowered to interpret and apply the law are authorized to appeal directly to the underlying morality in carrying out their duties. To the extent that the legal system functions as Dworkin thinks ours functions, the distinction between law and morality is blurred. Morality, or at least part of it, is absorbed into the law, and so there are fewer cases in which the two conflict.

But is it true that, in a good legal system, applying and interpreting the law will involve the kind of direct appeal to morality that will result in the requirements of both largely coinciding? There are reasons for thinking not. One reason for having a system of positive law backed by sanctions is that we do not expect sufficient voluntary compliance with morality. The problem, in legislating, is to find statutes that will increase the rate of compliance. When we can expect reasonable people to have difficulty determining whether specific acts accord with morality, or where it is easy to deceive oneself or others about the morality of one's conduct, it may well be desirable to have laws requiring more than what morality strictly requires. (I have suggested that such considerations may apply in the case of prohibitions on censorship and prohibitions on euthanasia.) But, while these considerations are relevant in the first instance to the task of legislating, they are also relevant to judicial decisions. The way that cases are decided will presumably affect the deterrent force of the law and, given the role of precedent in a system like ours, it can affect what the law *is*. Suppose we grant Dworkin's point that the moral considerations underlying the law are sometimes properly relevant to the law's interpretation — that the law cannot even be completely understood independent of an understanding of its moral function. It does not follow that the requirements of the law, properly interpreted, must coincide with the requirements of morality. There remains the question *how* the judge interpreting the law should take into account its moral basis. A plausible suggestion, in line with my argument up to this point, is that a judge interpreting the law should appeal to underlying moral considerations in roughly the way in which a good legislator should appeal to these considerations. He should ask

143

not simply 'what does morality say about this case?', but, 'given that this moral principle specifies the purpose of this law, how is the law to be interpreted so that it will serve to promote compliance with this principle?' In general, then, I would argue thus: If the arguments in Sections 1 and 2 are sound, laws requiring more than morality requires will sometimes be morally justifiable. For the same reasons, even if judges should sometimes appeal to morality in interpreting and applying the law, their interpretation should sometimes result in a law diverging from morality in the ways described.

2 I have talked some about the kinds of consideration — concern about possible abuse or unintentional misapplication for example — that are relevant in designing laws. It is because these considerations are relevant that I think the requirements of good laws will sometimes diverge from those of morality. But clearly the extent of the divergence will depend not only on how we conceive legislation (and the interpretation and application of the law) but also on how we conceive morality.

The idea behind at least some laws is to promote compliance with moral principles. If people comply with these laws they will act more morally than they would in the absence of the laws. Moral principles direct us to act so as to promote the goals and protect the interests and values around which a morality is structured. Roughly, then, moral principles and (some) laws tell us what to do to achieve the goals of morality. Since moral principles have roughly the same function as some laws, one would expect that they would coincide, but then my specification of this function has so far been most imprecise and vague. While I doubt that my characterization of this function will be much disputed, it is important in light of the problem I am discussing here that we consider more carefully how this characterization is to be understood.

This question has received some attention among writers who have worked on utilitarianism. Utilitarianism is structured around the goal of maximizing happiness. What does it mean, in the case of utilitarianism, to say that a principle tells us what to do to achieve the goals of morality?[15] Should a principle satisfy condition (1) or condition (2)?

1 Each act of compliance with the rule produces as much happiness as any alternative act would have produced.
2 If everyone were to follow the rule, maximum total happiness would result.

AU satisfies condition (1), but not condition (2) since there are situations in which compliance with rules other than AU results in increasing marginal returns as more and more people comply.[16] Sartorius evidently thinks the first condition gives the correct account of the sense in which a moral principle should promote the goals of morality. But, just because AU does not satisfy the second condition, a legislator following AU and in a position to determine what many people will do, will make laws requiring that people act in ways incompatible with AU. The point is this: There can be more than one plausible statement of the condition a principle must satisfy if it is to direct us to achieve the goals of morality. Given some conception of these goals, one way of understanding this condition will lead us to adopt one set of principles while another way of understanding it will lead us to adopt another set of principles. (In the case of utilitarianism, the most natural way to understand 'promotes the goals of morality' when one is talking about individual conduct is different from the most natural way to understand it when one speaks of legislation promoting those goals. This is part of the reason why morally good legislation is likely to diverge from the requirements of morality for individuals for a utilitarian.)

Quite apart from problems occasioned by theories built around the goal of maximizing some good, it is still possible to offer conflicting accounts of what it means for a principle to direct people to promote the goals and values of morality. Is a moral principle a principle such that

3 if people correctly act on it in light of a correct appreciation of the relevant facts each person will do the right thing

or is it a principle such that

4 if ordinary, fallible and biased people attempt to act on it, or to appear to act on it, each will do the right thing at least as often as he would attempting to act on (or appear to act on) any other principle?

I have clearly been assuming throughout that condition (4) was the appropriate one for at least some laws. One reason for having laws is that we do not expect adequate compliance with the requirements of morality in their absence. But if it is easy to pretend compliance with a law, in a case in which one is actually violating both the law and moral principle, then the law is not serving its purpose. (This again is just the sort of point Mrs Foot seems to be making about laws governing euthanasia.) But it is not at all clear that condition (4) is appropriate for morality. We can think of this in various ways. One might say that moral principles are supposed to tell us what actually is right — to offer us a criterion by which we can identify right acts. After all, if the purpose of some social or legal rules is to provide a standard of conduct that will lead, *practically*, to performance of acts that are *actually* right, we can test such rules only if there is some rule by which we can identify these actually right acts. Moral rules are these latter rules. When we make laws, we assume fallibility and limited good will on the part of those to whom the laws are addressed. When we consider what morality requires, we imagine people of good will with correct beliefs. We want principles satisfying condition (3).

The argument here is not conclusive, though the tentative conclusion is central to my claims about the relation between the requirements of law and the requirements of morality. If we assume that a correct moral principle is one satisfying condition (3) and that a law satisfying condition (4) but not condition (3) is sometimes morally justified, then it is likely that the requirements of a good law will sometimes diverge from the requirements of the moral principles on which laws are based. If we wish to evaluate this conclusion at greater length, it seems to me, what we need is a more serious investigation of just what conditions a correct moral principle must satisfy, of what its proper function is.[17]

4 SECONDARY PRINCIPLES OF OBLIGATION

In Section 1, I suggested some intuitive arguments for the view that justifiable laws may require more of us than do the moral principles on which they are based. In Section 2, I described a specifically utilitarian argument for the same conclusion and noted the natural utilitarian response, namely, that there is sometimes no moral obligation to comply with morally justified laws. In Section 3, I noted the way in which my conclusion depends on both an assumption about how laws should be interpreted and an assumption about the function of moral principles. If we give up either of the relevant assumptions it will be less likely that good laws and moral principles will diverge and it will be easier to justify an obligation to comply with good laws. In each case, however, I offered reasons for retaining the assumptions. In this section, I assume that justifiable laws will sometimes require more than the principles on which they are based, but I consider the possibility that there are other moral principles requiring us to comply with morally

justifiable laws. If there are such principles, the interesting question will
be whether they justify not only an obligation to comply with specific
justifiable laws, but also an obligation to comply with the outcome of
justifiable but imperfect social decision procedures – with the laws, for
example, adopted by a democratic legislature.

According to John Rawls, there are two moral principles from which
we can derive a duty or obligation to obey the law in a fundamentally
just (or near just) society. These principles are the natural duty of justice and the principle of fairness.[18] (Although several philosophers have
proposed principles similar to these,[19] and Rawls derives his statement
of the principle from these earlier proposals, I shall sometimes refer to
them, for convenience, as 'Rawls's principles'.) The natural duty of
justice 'requires us to support and to comply with just institutions that
exist and apply to us.' It also requires us 'to further just arrangements
not yet established, at least when this can be done without too much
cost to ourselves.' The general idea behind the first part of this duty is
that 'if the basic structure of society is just, or as just as it is reasonable
to expect in the circumstances, everyone has a natural duty to do his
part in the existing scheme' (Rawls, 115, cf. 334). According to the
principle of fairness,

> a person is required to do his part as defined by the rules of an insti-
> tution when . . . first, the institution is just (or fair) . . . and, second,
> one has voluntarily accepted the benefits of the arrangement or
> taken advantage of the opportunities it offers to further one's inter-
> ests. . . . when a number of persons engage in a mutually advantage-
> ous cooperative venture according to rules and thus restrict their
> liberty in ways necessary to yield advantages for all, those who have
> submitted to these restrictions have a right to a similar acquiescence
> on the part of those who have benefited from their submission
> (112, cf. 342-3).

The natural duty of justice generates duties, whereas the principle of
fairness generates obligations, in the narrow sense of this term. One's
obligations, as opposed to one's duties, depend on one's voluntary acts.
Thus, one can have a duty under the former principle without having an
obligation based on fairness. One has an obligation based on fairness
only if one takes some special, voluntary step to gain certain advantages
for oneself. For my purposes, however, what is important is the similarities between the principles, not the differences. According to each
principle, if basic laws and institutions are just, one has a duty (or obli-

gation) to do one's part in the system, and that means, in turn, that one must obey the law when it applies to one. One is required to comply regardless of whether (1) compliance in the specific case in question is independently required by some moral principle, (2) compliance in that particular case is strictly necessary for some goal on which the law is based, or (3) the particular law in question is even consistent with standards of justice or morality. The idea is that one makes a judgment about the justice or desirability of the system as a whole. Given that it is just as a whole, doing one's part is interpreted as requiring compliance with, so to speak, all of its parts.[20] Rawls makes this especially clear in an early paper, 'Legal Obligation and the Duty of Fair Play', in which he speaks of the principle of fairness applying to cooperative endeavors in which 'benefits are free'.[21] These are endeavors in which some level of cooperation is necessary for the production of a shared benefit, but universal cooperation is not necessary. In Rawls's view, each person must do his part even when, if some small number were 'free-riders', total benefits available would not diminish significantly.

Now, if we accept something like Rawls's principles, it appears that we will be required to comply with the law in spite of the various ways in which law may diverge from the requirements of moral principles so long as the system as a whole is justifiable. Of course, it is open to question whether we ought to accept such principles. Like other moral principles, we must ultimately seek their rationale in some reasonable conception of basic human needs and interests. I shall suggest some considerations in favor of some version of these principles in what follows. Whether they can be fully defended, however, will depend in part on just how they are interpreted. For my purposes, the question is whether, on a defensible interpretation, they will require compliance with the law in the full range of problematic cases I have discussed.

Principles like the principle of fairness and the natural duty of justice may seem strange in more than one way. On the one hand, they may seem redundant − they may seem to require conduct already required by other principles. On the other hand, they may seem to require just the wrong kind of thing in those areas in which they are not redundant. In the following pages I shall take up, first, the question of the principles' redundancy and, second, the question whether they require too much.

It is doubtful, I shall argue later, that a plausible version of Rawls's principles will require obedience in the whole range of cases in which there is question about the obligation to obey the law. On the other hand, there are a number of cases in which it seems intuitively, that people are obligated to obey the law and in which it is hard to explain that obligation without reference to principles something like these. Hence, the principles are not obviously redundant. One kind of case is the case in which a law is designed to produce benefits not required by morality. In some such cases, the benefits are produced only if there is widespread compliance with the law, but each individual act of compliance is not necessarily required. These are the cases in which, in Rawls's phrase, the benefits of cooperation are 'free'. Individuals will be tempted not to do their part, and there is no independent moral requirement that the benefits be produced, but it does seem natural to say that people who enjoy the benefits ought to cooperate in their production.

Another kind of law is of even greater interest. So far, when I have spoken of the laws and institutions required by morality, I have spoken of laws that more or less correspond to moral principles applying to individuals — laws against assault, for example. (Some of the problems I have mentioned about political obligation arise because laws rationally based on these principles of individual conduct require *more* than these principles themselves.) However, we may need to distinguish moral principles for individuals and moral principles for institutions. When institutions are just it is not merely because they effectively enforce various principles of individual morality, but also because they satisfy the requirements of principles for institutions. Such principles may require that laws and institutions taken together tend to have certain consequences, e.g., that they tend to be efficient in the production of certain goods, that they lead to a fair distribution of these goods, or that they respect certain freedoms. Individual laws and institutions do not satisfy the requirements of these principles by themselves. What determines the acceptability of a system is the way in which various laws work together to produce desired results, or, better, the way in which *general compliance with* the whole system of laws leads to these results.

Given the conception of morally good laws just presented, there will be many situations in which noncompliance with a good law will not be wrong *in itself*. First, whether it is wrong will depend on the presence or absence of background institutions. (Different sets of laws may be functionally equivalent so that a law that is good within one system may be bad within another.) Second, even given appropriate background laws and institutions, what is important is a high level of compliance throughout the society. Compliance by one individual (or a small group) would not be sufficient to produce good results. *Universal* compliance might not be necessary. The effects of compliance with many tax laws may illustrate both these points. If most people pay their taxes, and the tax revenues are designated for certain purposes, and there is no graft, then the system may satisfy one of the conditions necessary for a system's being just. (An example might be taxation used to finance a system of public education which, in turn, advances the ideal of equal opportunity.)

Both in the case of laws promoting a collective benefit, morally permitted but not required, and in the case of a system of laws designed to achieve some purpose morally necessary if the system is to be just, any obligation to obey the law cannot be explained except by reference to some principle of obligation other than the kind of principle which applies to individuals independent of society. If compliance with the kind of tax law just described is required, it is not required in the way, or for the reason, that compliance with a law prohibiting assault is required. No act of compliance with the tax laws is either necessary or sufficient for any morally good result, though general compliance is. Yet we are inclined to say — at least I am — that those who enjoy collective goods should cooperate in the production of those goods, and those who benefit from society generally should contribute their fair share of the sacrifices necessary to make society just. Compliance with the natural duty of justice and the principle of fair play, it would seem, results in an appropriate distribution of the benefits and burdens of social life, and it also produces various required and otherwise desirable results.

I have not offered a precise statement of the natural duty of justice or the principle of fairness, and I have also not offered a thorough justification for them. Indeed, serious questions remain about their ultimate acceptability.[22] I have attempted to reply to the objection that they are redundant in the sense that what they require is clearly required on independent grounds anyhow. There remains the question whether they require too much. As Rawls evidently understands these principles, they would require that we cooperate in the pursuit of public benefits, and that we do things like paying our taxes when a tax is part of a system of laws and institutions that work together to produce some morally required result. But he also takes them to require compliance with the law in general, even in the kinds of problematic cases we have discussed earlier. Thus, we ought to comply with the law when a generally just democratic process produces a law in conflict with morality. Also, though he does not discuss this case explicitly, when a statute or constitutional amendment forbids certain conduct on the ground of possible abuse, Rawls might say that it should be obeyed even in a case that does not involve any *actual* abuse. But now the question is whether, given a defensible interpretation of Rawls's principles, they will actually require compliance in cases like these.

Rawls's principles, even in their most obvious applications, require us to comply with generally beneficial rules even when our particular contribution is of negligible importance. Critics of the principles will naturally object to them on just this ground: they require unnecessary, wasteful sacrifice.[23] How might a defender of the principles reply? While admitting that less than universal cooperation is sometimes sufficient for the benefits of cooperation, he could reply that the individual acts of cooperation required are not relevantly different from one another and that, in fairness, if anyone should cooperate, all should.

The objection that Rawls's principles require unnecessary and wasteful sacrifice, I believe, needs to be taken seriously; and I also believe that the reply I suggested is at least plausible. As it stands, however, this reply is incomplete. If the defender of the principles claims that the required acts of cooperation are all relevantly similar, and therefore that it is not irrational to require all of them, he must provide a criterion of relevant similarity. I shall suggest a criterion in terms of what I call the *causal relevance* of an act to the production of a shared benefit or good. I shall then argue, however, that if Rawls's principles require only those acts causally relevant in this way, these principles will not require general compliance with all the laws — even all the good laws — in a just or near just democracy. The account of causal relevance is as follows.

Take any rule R general compliance with which will produce good results. We can imagine some other rule, R', requiring just what R requires, but also imposing some silly extra requirement on a few people. (All those born on February 29, between 10:00 and 10:10 must include in their income tax return one blade of grass.) If compliance with R' will produce just the same goods, in the same quantity, that compliance with R will produce, it is tempting to say that compliance with R is all that is morally required. A plausible version of the principle of fairness or the natural duty of justice, it seems to me, will require no more than this, since the additional acts required by R' are irrelevant. The sense in which they are irrelevant is that they are causally unrelated to the production of the benefits in question. A person's act, A, is causally relevant to the production of some good, I shall say, just in case either (1) there is some number of people such that, if they cooperate, A is causally sufficient to produce at least some of the good, or (2) there is some number of people such that, if they cooperate, A is causally necessary to produce some of the good.

I am not certain that this account of causal relevance is adequate. The general idea is to distinguish those acts that actually contribute to production of social goods from those acts that do not contribute at all. The problem is that we are dealing with situations in which, at least often, no particular act is by itself either necessary or sufficient for the production of the good in question. However, if we take Rawls's principles to require cooperation only when an act of cooperation is causally relevant in my sense, they may require cooperation even when, given the *actual* level of cooperation, cooperation is not necessary. They may also require cooperation when, under some imaginable circumstances (if the actual level of cooperation were below some threshold), it would produce nothing. Still, the principles will not require compliance with something like the blade of grass rule mentioned above. More interesting, they will not require compliance with some of the problematic laws I have discussed in earlier parts of this chapter. Consider the general prohibition on infanticide. This is designed to prevent *unjustifiable* infanticides. But if, as Mrs Foot has suggested, some infanticides would be cases of *justifiable* euthanasia, those infanticides would not be causally relevant to the goals of the law. Hence, on the interpretation of Rawls's principles under consideration, compliance with the law in all cases would not be required. Nor, of course, will compliance be required in those cases in which a law serves no good purpose at all. Hence, Rawls's principles as interpreted will not necessarily require compliance with all laws in a democracy.

I have argued that Rawls's principles do not necessarily require (even presumptively) that we comply with all laws in a just democracy. More precisely, I have argued that we are not required to comply in virtue of the *content* of the laws we can expect to find in a just democracy. Acts of compliance, even with good laws, are not always, in virtue of their content, either good in themselves or causally relevant to the production of some shared benefit. But it might be replied that I have neglected an important way in which compliance with laws results in general benefits. Roughly, the idea is that having an authoritative social decision procedure is itself socially useful regardless of the content of its decisions. But it is useful just to the extent that it is generally accepted as authoritative, and that means that it must be complied with. Every instance of compliance, however, will be relevant to the benefits derived from having a procedure at all.

Two kinds of situation seem to suggest this reply. First, consider rules of the road. Within broad limits, it does not matter what these rules are as long as some rules are commonly acknowledged and obeyed. Uniformity is important, but any uniformity will do. An easy way to achieve uniformity in the many different driving situations requiring uniform behavior is to have a single second order uniformity: everyone acknowledges the authority of some rule-making body and complies with it. Second, consider procedures for settling disputes. Suppose people have frequent disputes, they cannot agree on principles that will settle them, and they care enough about having them settled that they cannot get on with the general business of living until they are settled. Possibly, though for every settled dispute there will be someone who loses, everyone would gain on balance if each would acknowledge the authority of some common dispute-settling procedure.

It is tempting to generalize from situations like these and conclude that compliance with the outcome of common decision procedures is always relevant to some common benefit. Any decision, regardless of its content, is better than none. I say this is tempting, but I think it is a mistake. The situations I have described are situations in which there is a need for some kind of coordination. It is desirable that government make a law or a decision in order to facilitate coordination. Even if coordination or a resolution of a dispute is possible without government, an authoritative governmental decision makes it easier. Moreover, compliance with the government's decision is at least causally relevant to the achievement of desired coordination or to the smooth resolution of preexisting disputes. But some governmental decisions do not have these effects. Laws can have purposes other than the promotion of independently needed coordination, and compliance with these other laws is not necessarily relevant to the goal of coordination. In short, we have again found reason to say that compliance with collective decision procedures is causally relevant to the production of shared benefits — and is therefore required by Rawls's principles — only in the case of a subclass of such decisions.

CONCLUDING REMARKS

In exploring possible justifications for democracy I have favored those that focus on the likely quality of its legislation, and not on the obligation, if any, to obey its laws. I have favored these justifications partly because the quality of a government's laws seems to me clearly an important consideration. I have preferred these justifications also because it is my conviction that the question whether we have an obligation to obey the law is fundamentally a question of individual morality. If we do have such an obligation it is at least partly because moral principles of individual conduct require obedience. There is no form of government which, in virtue of its form *alone*, generates obligatory legislation. If we have an obligation to obey the law, it will be, again, partly in virtue of what moral principles require of us. If there are moral principles generating a general obligation of obedience, I suspect, there will be some range of governmental forms within which they will apply. Within this range, the interesting differences between governmental forms will not be differences in legitimacy, if legitimacy is understood to involve a general obligation to obey the law.

From the claim that our obligations to obey the law are obligations we have in virtue of some moral principle it does not *follow* that our having these obligations is not conditional on the form of government. Whether it does depend on the form of government depends on the content of the moral principles in question. In Chapters II, III and IV, indeed, I considered briefly moral principles, or construals of moral principles, according to which one would have a special obligation to obey the law as a consequence of the form of government. I rejected these principles. In this chapter I have looked at a number of questions about the nature of moral principles governing individual conduct, about the nature of morally good laws and morally good legal and political systems, and about two specific principles of obligation. I have concluded, at least tentatively, that there is no automatic obligation to obey all laws in a democracy and, indeed, that there is no moral obligation to comply with at least some of the directives of morally good laws.

These two points are connected. If it seems strange that a procedure could be justifiable *and* that it is permissible to disregard its outcome, it may at least seem less strange if it is possible for a *law* to be a good law though some of its requirements are not obligatory. If even good laws are not obligatory in every instance, who would expect good decision procedures always to yield binding decisions? That is the rhetorical connection between the two points. They are also connected in that they have the same explanation, and the explanation takes us back to the questions raised in Chapter I, basic questions about the function of government and about its permissibility. I have argued in favor of a kind of democracy on the assumption that it is morally permissible to have a system of government in the first place. I have not defended this latter assumption except to suggest that it is useful in various respects to have a system of laws and a procedure for making and changing those laws. A system of government can promote compliance with the requirements of morality, and it can coordinate people's behavior in mutually beneficial ways. On balance, it may do more good than harm. A good system, moreover, will tend to pass laws consistent with the requirements of morality. This kind of pragmatic argument for having a government — the argument that, on balance, it will do more good than harm — is analogous to the kind of argument that can be given for particular laws, including laws based directly on moral principles and designed to promote compliance with those principles. If this kind of justification is what one has in mind when one says we are justified in having a government or a certain law, it is certainly not inconsistent for him to deny that the requirements of a government, or a good law, are always morally binding.

The overall structure of my view, then, is something like this: the first question is whether we are permitted to have a coercive government at all, and the answer is that we are permitted to have one if it will produce more good than harm. Given that there are permissible governments, we are further constrained to find the type of government that will produce the most good or the least harm. (I have offered reasons to think that, in terms of moral good and harm, this type of government is democracy.) A good system of government achieves its goal of producing good and preventing harm by adopting laws and policies which, in turn, produce maximum benefits with minimum cost. But, minimum cost is not no cost at all. At the very least, a good government may sometimes require us — coerce us — to do things that we are not morally required to do. The correct response, I think, is *not* that the government is therefore not justifiable, and it is *not* that, since it is justifiable, we must be morally required to comply with its directives in every case. The correct response, rather, is that *sometimes* we are permitted to disobey the law in a good state.

What I have just said, however, must be qualified in one important respect. I have spoken, vaguely, of maximizing benefits and minimizing harms. One might reply that any harm — any limitation on freedom that does not coincide directly with a moral constraint, for example — is sufficient to render a government unjustifiable. This is the anarchist response. A weaker response is that *some* harms, *some* restrictions on liberty are sufficient to render a government unjustifiable. I am inclined to accept this view. I suspect there are some rights which people have independent of the state and which no state may violate. I also suspect that, if we are to have a coercive state at all, it must satisfy certain conditions if it is to be justifiable. Some harms and some benefits are more important than others. The case for democracy is simply that it is more likely than other types of system to respond to these differences in degree of importance, and to respect the more fundamental rights and interests.

NOTES

INTRODUCTION

1 That questions of definition, evaluation and feasibility are interrelated, and that we should therefore consider whole theories of democracy instead of one or another type of question in isolation, seems to me an important methodological directive. It stands quite independent of any of the substantive points I shall make later. I have not seen this point made in connection with democratic theory generally, through Arthur Kuflik has made a similar point in a discussion of majority rule. See 'Majority Rule Procedure' in *Due Process, Nomos XVIII*, J. R. Pennock and J. W. Chapman, eds (New York, New York University Press, 1977), 296-332.

Readers of Robert Dahl's *Preface to Democratic Theory* (Chicago, University of Chicago Press, 1956) may find familiar the idea of comparing and contrasting various different theories of democracy. I find this book confusing, though, since I have trouble telling whether his different theories of democracy are different justifications of the same thing or different definitions of democracy.

I DECISIONS AND PROCEDURES

1 I am speaking here of decision *tokens* — particular decisions, not types of decision — since it is doubtful that there is any type of decision each instance of which is always other-regarding or not other-regarding. (I except the last two types mentioned as degenerate cases.) Also, I use 'decision' broadly to include those decisions we make by not deciding in cases of forced choice. Finally, I include decisions that get made by social processes like convention, or by the market and similar 'invisible hand mechanisms'. On these last two categories, see David Lewis, *Convention* (Cambridge, Mass.,

Harvard University Press, 1969), Ch. 1-3, and Robert Nozick, *Anarchy, State and Utopia* (New York, Basic Books, 1974), 18-22.

2 Carl Cohen, in *Democracy* (Athens, Ga., University of Georgia Press, 1971), seems to think that, at least in a democracy, every decision should be made by the participation of everyone affected. See his Chapters 2 and 15, and see Chapter III, Section 5 below.

3 See Lewis, *op. cit.*

4 See R. Duncan Luce and Howard Raiffa, *Games and Decisions* (New York, Wiley, 1957), Ch. 5.

5 John Locke, *Second Treatise of Civil Government*, Sections 13, 123-31.

6 This problem will be familiar to readers of Mill's *On Liberty*. Mill seems to argue that the state can interfere only with those acts which can be expected to cause harm to others. But there seems to be almost no *type* of act that is purely private in the sense that no instance of that type causes harm for others. Hence, it seems that Mill's limitation on government excludes almost no laws.

7 Nozick, in *Anarchy, State and Utopia* (*op. cit.*), seems to take the Lockean view that the state is justified only in enforcing pre-political moral principles, but he says very little about how the legislative system — much less the judicial system — will work. Will there be promulgated law? Will the judicial system respect precedent? Won't these sometimes depart from natural morality, and will the judicial system take into account innocently formed expectations based on errant laws and precedents? Shouldn't it?

8 Hobbes, *Leviathan*, Chapter 21.

9 Compare Nozick's useful remarks on legitimacy in *Anarchy, State and Utopia, op. cit.*, 133ff.

10 *Ibid.*, Ch. 7. Nozick's 'historical' theory of justice incorporates a theory of natural rights something like Locke's. He contrasts this kind of theory with the more common modern theory represented by Rawls's *A Theory of Justice* (Cambridge, Mass., Harvard University Press, 1971).

11 On the place of procedural rights in morality generally, see Nozick, *op. cit.*, 96ff. On the inadequacy of democratic legislative procedures in particular, given the demands of morality, see the classic paper by Richard Wollheim, 'A Paradox in the Theory of Democracy', in Laslett and Runciman, eds, *Philosophy, Politics and Society*, 2nd series (Oxford, Blackwell, 1962) and R. P. Wolff, *In Defense of Anarchism* (New York, Harper & Row, 1970). For a social scientist's criticism of democratic procedures because of their results, see George D. Beam, *Usual Politics* (New York, Holt, Rinehart & Winston, 1970).

II PROCEDURAL FAIRNESS AND EQUALITY

1 For one thing, this definition is framed in terms of complete social

states. It is possible that social state A is preferred by a majority to social state B even though social state B would be selected as a result of majority voting on individual issues taken one at a time. See Anthony Downs, *An Economic Theory of Democracy* (New York, Harper & Row, 1957), 55ff., and R. Dahl, *A Preface to Democratic Theory* (Chicago, University of Chicago Press, 1956), Ch. 2, for a variety of problems about implementing majority rule.

2 See A. K. Sen, *Collective Choice and Social Welfare* (San Francisco, Holden Day, 1970), 23, 28.

3 *Ibid.*, 68, 71-3. Sen states the conditions formally and proves the result.

4 Note that our requirement of a 2/3 majority for a constitutional amendment seems to violate neutrality. I suspect that is why John Rawls regards such requirements as 'limitations on the principle of participation' and claims that they require special justification. See *A Theory of Justice* (Cambridge, Mass., Harvard University Press, 1971), Sec. 37.

5 Rawls, *op. cit.*, sometimes seems to argue for democracy by direct appeal to his first principle of justice requiring 'equal liberties'. See, e.g., Section 36, but contrast Sections 31 and 54 in which he regards the justification of democracy as a case of imperfect procedural justice. Carl Cohen, in *Democracy* (Athens, Ga., University of Georgia Press, 1971), argues for democracy in terms of its intrinsic equality in Chapter 15, and Dahl (*op. cit.*, Ch. 2) takes seriously the idea of 'political equality' as an end in itself.

6 Peter Singer, *Democracy and Disobedience* (New York, Oxford University Press, 1973). Subsequent references in the text to Singer are to this volume.

7 The distinction here is the distinction between different aspects of legitimacy, especially the distinction between 'the right to rule' and 'ruling rightly', drawn in Chapter I. For further discussion of 'the right to rule', see Section 4 of this chapter, and Chapter VII below.

8 Singer does eventually take up the question of the fair *operation* of a decision procedure, and he seems to conclude that fair operation is also important (Singer, 44, 45). But what are we to make of this? Is his earlier argument now irrelevant?

9 Rawls, *op. cit.*, p. 85. For the sake of argument, I shall assume here that Rawls's conception of pure procedural justice is unproblematic, and see how far that takes us. For a more fundamental critique, see William Nelson, 'The Very Idea of Pure Procedural Justice', *Ethics*, forthcoming.

10 See J. Buchanan and G. Tullock, *The Calculus of Consent* (Ann Arbor, University of Michigan Press, 1962). I shall discuss this kind of theory in Chapter V below.

11 This seems to be Rawls's considered view. See *A Theory of Justice*, *op. cit.*, Sections 31 and 54.

12 Robert Nozick, *Anarchy, State and Utopia* (New York, Basic Books, 1974), Chapter 7, Section I.

13 *Ibid.*, 150-3.
14 I do not mean to suggest that Nozick would accept this argument for democracy. He says very little about governmental decision procedures, and he would surely agree that the outcome of these procedures is important to their evaluation.
15 For an argument something like this, see Carl Cohen, *op. cit.* Democracy, he says, is government in which members of the community participate. He seems to think further that, if people participate in government they are self governing, and that self government (autonomy) is an intrinsic good.
16 As I have noted, Rawls argues for majority rule in other sections of the text. He seems to assume something like different branches of a legislature, one of which will deal with questions involving justice and morality, another of which will deal with public goods and will operate on a rule of unanimity.

   Some of the properties of majority and unanimity rule relevant to the discussion here will be examined in Chapter V. In Chapter VI, I defend a form of representative government operating on majority rule. I assume it will deal with matters of substantive morality as well as public goods legislation. For the latter, I agree that there are some advantages to the idea of unanimity. However, I see no obvious way to devise two distinct branches of government and then assign just the right kind of decision to each. Under either kind of rule, in any case, I argue that an *open* government will be constrained not to alter institutions required by morality.
17 Here I interpret Rawls's theory as a (constrained) entitlement theory in Nozick's sense of the term (see note 12 above). See also, William Nelson, 'The Very Idea of Pure Procedural Justice', *op. cit.*
18 It is curious, incidentally, that Rawls does not discuss this case in Section 37 where he discusses other 'limitations on the principle of participation'.
19 See H. L. A. Hart, 'Are There Any Natural Rights?', *Philosophical Review*, LXIV, No 2 (April 1955), 185, and John Rawls, *op. cit.*, Section 52.
20 See Nozick, *op. cit.*, 95.

III PARTICIPATION

1 See Donald W. Keim, 'Participation in Contemporary Democratic Theories', in *Nomos XVI, Participation in Politics* (New York, Lieber-Atherton, 1975), 1-38.
2 J. Schumpeter, *Capitalism, Socialism and Democracy*, 3rd edn (New York, Harper & Row, 1950).
3 *Ibid.*, 250.
4 I shall consider other types of argument for popular sovereignty in Chapter IV.
5 Schumpeter, *op. cit.*, 269.

6 In using this term I follow a number of recent theorists, in particular, Henry S. Kariel in his anthology *Frontiers of Democratic Theory* (New York, Random House, 1970).

7 Reprinted as 'Normative Consequences of Democratic Theory' in Henry S. Kariel (ed.), *op. cit.*, 227-47 (references are to this edition). This anthology contains a number of interesting selections from the work of revisionists, and from that of their critics. Among the critics, one should also see, especially, Peter Bachrach, *The Theory of Democratic Elitism* (Boston, Little Brown, 1967).

8 Walker, *ibid.*, 228.

9 *Ibid.*, 232.

10 See Robert Dahl's reply to Walker, 'Further Reflections on "the Elitist Theory of Democracy" ', *American Political Science Review*, LX, No. 2 (June 1966), 296-305.

11 Walker, *op. cit.*, 227.

12 Compare Bachrach, *op. cit.*, 86.

13 Carole Pateman, *Participation and Democratic Theory* (Cambridge, Cambridge University Press, 1970).

14 *Ibid.*, 17.

15 *Ibid.*, 18-20.

16 *Ibid.*, 20.

17 *Ibid.*, 37, 43. The idea of a participatory society may well be something like what Bachrach is getting at in the concluding pages of his book, *op. cit.*, 102ff.

18 Pateman, *op. cit.*, 109-111, and Bachrach, *op. cit.*, many references, e.g. pp. 1, 95. This point may help to explain the exasperation of writers like Robert Dahl in his reply to Walker, *op. cit.*, in *After the Revolution* (New Haven, Yale University Press, 1970), and 'Democracy and the Chinese Boxes', reprinted in Kariel, ed., *op. cit.*, 370-93.

19 See Samuel P. Huntington, 'The Democratic Distemper', *The Public Interest*, No. 41, Fall, 1975, 9-38, and Robert Dahl, *A Preface to Democratic Theory* (Chicago, University of Chicago Press, 1956), 87-9.

20 Walker, *op. cit.*, Sec. 2.

21 See Pateman, *op. cit.*, 70-1, for a brief discussion of degrees of power and influence. On self government and autonomy in connection with participation theory see Carl Cohen, *Democracy* (Athens, Ga., University of Georgia Press, 1971), 4-5, 6, and Chapter 16. See also John Ladd, 'The Ethics of Participation', in *Nomos XVI, Participation in Politics, op. cit.*, 98-135.

22 See Huntington, *op. cit.*, and the selection from Lester Milbrath's *Political Participation* reprinted in Kariel, ed., *op. cit.*, 81-9.

23 Pateman, *op. cit.*, 27, 63-4, 74-5.

24 See Robert Paul Wolff, *In Defense of Anarchism* (New York, Harper & Row, 1970).

25 Thomas Hobbes, *Leviathan*, Chapters 14, 16, 17. For more recent work, see John Plamenatz, *Consent, Freedom and Political Obliga-*

tion, 2nd edn. (London, Oxford University Press, 1968), and Hannah Pitkin, *The Concept of Representation* (Berkeley, Ca., University of California Press, 1967), Ch. 1-3

26 For some interesting observations on the relation between consent and other acts that generate obligations see A. John Simmons, 'Tacit Consent and Political Obligation', *Philosophy and Public Affairs*, 5, no. 3 (Spring 1976), 274-91.

27 P. Singer, *Democracy and Disobedience* (New York, Oxford University Press, 1973).

28 *Ibid.,* 45-59, esp. 52-3. See also Simmons, *op. cit.,* 289. Contrast Plamenatz, *op. cit.,* 168, 170, quoted in Simmons.

29 *Ibid.,* 49-53.

30 *Ibid.,* 51.

31 See, for example, Carl Cohen, *op. cit.,* 16-17, and Sec. 15.3.

32 Compare R. Nozick, *Anarchy, State and Utopia* (New York, Basic Books, 1974), 238.

33 Cohen, *op. cit.,* Sec. 15.3.

34 This view is expressed forcefully in Hannah Arendt, *On Revolution* (New York, Viking, 1963), 65.

35 See Bachrach, *The Theory of Democratic Elitism, op. cit.,* 98; and 'Interest, Participation and Democratic Theory', in *Nomos XVI, Participation in Politics, op. cit.,* 39-55.

36 J. S. Mill, *Considerations on Representative Government* (Indianapolis and New York, Bobbs-Merrill, 1958), 25.

37 Pateman, *op. cit.,* 24-5, 29-31, 45-6, 63-4, 74.

38 Pateman herself, it should be noted, is not so much interested in questions of justification. Her main concern is with questions of feasibility.

39 Mill, *op. cit.,* 5-6, 15, 24-5.

IV POPULAR SOVEREIGNTY

1 Joseph Schumpeter, I think, is too quick in just this way. See *Capitalism, Socialism and Democracy,* 3rd edn (New York, Harper & Row, 1950), Ch. XXI, Secs 1-2.

2 Kenneth Arrow, *Social Choice and Individual Values,* 2nd edn (New York, Wiley, 1963). For my exposition, I shall rely primarily on the version of Arrow's proof in A. K. Sen, *Collective Choice and Social Welfare* (San Francisco, Holden Day, 1970).

3 I. M. D. Little suggests this interpretation in his review of Arrow, 'Social Choice and Individual Values', reprinted in E. S. Phelps, ed., *Economic Justice* (Baltimore, Penguin Books, 1973), see especially 140.

4 I take it that I disagree here with Robert Paul Wolff, *In Defense of Anarchism* (New York, Harper & Row, 1970), 59, 63.

5 For the following see Sen, *op. cit.,* Ch. 3*, especially 41-2.

6 Luce and Raiffa, *Games and Decisions* (New York, Wiley, 1957),

Ch. 14, Sec. 5.
7 Sen, *op. cit.*, 15, 47.
8 *Ibid.*, 47-8, 52-3.
9 S. I. Benn and R. S. Peters, *Principles of Political Thought* (Chicago, Free Press, 1959), 336.
10 *Ibid.*, 344.
11 See Robert Paul Wolff, *op. cit.*; Rousseau, *The Social Contract*, Bk I, Chs. 1, 3, 6; R. Wollheim, 'A Paradox in the Theory of Democracy' in Laslett and Runciman, eds, *Philosophy, Politics and Society*, 2nd Series (Oxford, Blackwell, 1962). It is not clear where a libertarian writer like Robert Nozick stands, or should stand, on the matter of the importance of the problem of political obligation. As he sees it, the state can tax only those who voluntarily submit to taxation, but it can punish anyone who violates the rights of its clients, even if the punished has no agreement with the state. With respect to some exercises of authority, then, the problem of legitimate authority for Nozick is different from that problem as it appears to Wolff or Wollheim. See *Anarchy, State and Utopia* (New York, Basic Books, 1974).
12 Wolff, *op. cit.*, especially 12-13.
13 See Buchanan and Tullock, *The Calculus of Consent* (Ann Arbor, University of Michigan Press, 1962), Chs. 12, 13, and A. K. Sen, *op. cit.*, 24-7.
14 Nozick, *op. cit.*, Ch. 10.
15 Sen, *op. cit.*, 26. The point here about the argument from liberty is reminiscent of the 'Paradox of liberalism' discussed by Sen in Chs. 6 and 6*. (For an informal exposition, see Nozick, *op. cit.*, 164-6.) Suppose we say that, for each of two persons, there is a pair of alternatives over which that person can determine the social choice. Suppose we also require that our social choice rule satisfy 'acyclicity' (a weak consistency condition similar to transitivity) and a unanimity condition (if everyone prefers x to y, then x is socially preferred to y). It turns out that no social decision rule can satisfy these requirements and also satisfy the condition of universal domain: it is possible to imagine some set of individual preferences such that the requirements of acyclicity, unanimity and individual rights are in conflict.
16 Wolff, *op. cit.*, seems to miss this point, since he seems to think that a unanimous, direct democracy, at least, would be legitimate (see 22-7). But such a system, if it functioned at all, would function by forcing people to *compromise* with one another in ways not obviously compatible with autonomy.
17 See Albert O. Hirschman, *Exit, Voice and Loyalty* (Cambridge, Mass., Harvard University Press, 1970).
18 Wolff, *op. cit.*, actually does say that a person acting autonomously could also be acting wrongly, which raises the question in what sense he thinks the principle of autonomy is really fundamental, see p. 13.

19 See Mancur Olson, *The Logic of Collective Action* (Cambridge, Mass., Harvard University Press, 1965, 1971).

20 See the discussion of Rawls's views on the pursuit of collective goods in Ch. II, Sec. 3, Sub. Sec. 3, and the discussion of Buchanan and Tullock's theory in Chapter V.

21 See B. J. Diggs, 'Practical Representation', in *Nomos X, Representation* (New York, Atherton, 1968), 29-30, 35-7; and Hannah Pitkin, *The Concept of Representation* (Berkeley and Los Angeles, University of California Press, 1967), Chs. 6, 7, 10. Pitkin suggests that, in general, when representing is acting, to represent is to *act for*. What this amounts to, however, differs depending on what is being represented. Thus, her account of representative government is broader. Her book also contains a good account of a variety of theories of representation.

22 See Pitkin, *op. cit.*, 215, 219ff.

23 Is it necessary that a representative be representative (typical) of his constituents? Must a representative assembly as a whole constitute a representation or sampling of the nation? (Pitkin, *op. cit.*, Ch. 4). What is the relevance of principles like the 'one man one vote' rule? See Charles L. Black, Jr, 'Representation in Law and Equity', *Nomos X, Representation, op. cit.*, e.g., 150-141 and see Stuart M. Brown, 'Black on Representation: A Question', in the same volume, 147-44.

24 Duncan Black, *The Theory of Committees and Elections* (Cambridge, Cambridge University Press, 1971), 19.

25 *Ibid.*, 39ff.

V ECONOMIC THEORIES

1 The general characterization of economic theories here is derived to some extent from Brian Barry, *Sociologists, Economists and Democracy* (London, Collier-Macmillan, 1970).

2 See Chapter II, Section 1, above.

3 See Robert Dahl, *Preface to Democratic Theory* (Chicago, University of Chicago Press, 1956), Ch. 4.

4 Anthony Downs, *An Economic Theory of Democracy* (New York, Harper & Row, 1957).

5 *Ibid.*, 54-5. This assumes majority rule, and it assumes political parties motivated solely by a desire to attain (or to keep) office. Both assumptions are basic to Downs's approach.

6 *Ibid.*, see 55-60 for a general account of conditions under which the minority coalition strategy will work.

7 Dahl argues that the problem of majority tyranny is mitigated by the fact that we do not have rule by 'monolithic majorities' in pluralistic societies, but rather what he calls 'minorities rule'. Dahl also hypothesizes that intense minorities derive some protection from the observed tendency of the apathetic not to vote. See Dahl,

op. cit., Ch. 5. It is useful to read Dahl's discussion of 'minorities rule' in conjunction with Downs's discussion of the majority principle and the possibility of minority coalitions.

8 James Buchanan and Gordon Tullock, *The Calculus of Consent* (Ann Arbor, Michigan, University of Michigan Press, 1962). Subsequent unidentified references in the text are to this volume.

9 *Ibid.*, 100-3, or see any elementary introduction to price theory.

10 Downs, *op. cit.*, 290ff.

11 Buchanan and Tullock tend to speak of *explaining* democratic constitutions instead of *justifying* them. But if the explanation postulates a set of conditions under which a democratic constitution would be chosen, the explanation converts to a justification if we also think that the choice conditions carry normative import — if we think that those conditions include the conditions which make a choice morally good.

12 For a contrary opinion see Mancur Olson's review of *The Calculus of Consent* in the *American Economic Review* for December 1962. See also Olson's book, *The Logic of Collective Action* (Cambridge, Mass., Harvard University Press, 1965, 1971).

13 See Robert Nozick, *Anarchy, State and Utopia* (New York, Basic Books, 1974), 150ff.

14 Downs, *op. cit.*, Chapter 10, Part II.

15 *Principles of Morals and Legislation*, Ch. 2, Para. 4.

16 See Thomas Scanlon, 'Preference and Urgency', *Journal of Philosophy*, LXXII, No. 19, November 6 1975, 655-99.

17 See, for example, Robert Dahl, *Pluralist Democracy in the United States* (Chicago, Rand McNally, 1967).

VI OPEN GOVERNMENT AND JUST LEGISLATION: A DEFENSE OF DEMOCRACY

1 Robert Dahl, *Preface to Democratic Theory* (Chicago, University of Chicago Press, 1956). (Subsequent references in the text to 'Dahl' are to this volume.)

2 Control of 'factions' is also supposed to be necessary, but that is irrelevant to my argument here.

3 We have seen that some of the participation theorists, as well as those with whom they disagree, have been concerned with the psychological prerequisites of stable, decent government. Some of the former, of course, argue that extensive participation contributes to the development of the relevant psychological conditions.

4 See Carl Hempel, 'Empiricist Criteria of Cognitive Significance: Problems and Changes' in his *Aspects of Scientific Explanation* (Chicago, Free Press, 1956).

5 It is supposed to be an advantage of the Pareto criterion that it makes conceptual demands weaker than those of some other welfare criteria, specifically those that presuppose interpersonal

comparisons of levels of utility. The Pareto criterion, unlike some others, *is* operational.

6 John Rawls, *A Theory of Justice* (Cambridge, Mass., Harvard University Press, 1971), 3.

7 Trivial examples include such rules as 'everyone stop on red and go on green'. Some examples are instances of coordination problems in which everyone gains *if and only if* everyone follows some rule. Other examples are analogous to the prisoners' dilemma in which universal cooperation is sufficient, but not necessary for the production of some shared benefit. The latter cases, of course, present serious problems of instability. For an interesting discussion of coordination problems, see David Lewis, *Convention* (Cambridge, Mass., Harvard University Press, 1969). For the prisoners' dilemma, see Luce and Raiffa, *Games and Decisions* (New York, Wiley, 1957), Ch. 5. On the relation between these problems and the requirements of morality, see David Gauthier, 'Morality and Advantage', *Philosophical Review*, LXXVI, No. 4 (October 1967), 460-75.

8 The so called 'Principle of Fairness' is an example of such a rule. See Rawls, *op. cit.*, Section 18.

9 Rawls, *op. cit.*, 5. (Subsequent references in the text to 'Rawls' are to this volume.)

10 Among modern writers, Rawls is the best known proponent of a kind of hypothetical contract theory, though there are others. Gilbert Harman conceives of morality as a kind of actual agreement among actual persons. See 'Moral Relativism Defended', *Philosophical Review*, LXXXIV, No. 1 (January 1975); *The Nature of Morality* (New York, Oxford University Press, 1977), Chs. 5-8; and 'Relativistic Ethics: Morality as Politics', *Midwest Studies in Philosophy*, III (University of Minnesota, Morris, 1978), 109-21.

11 Thomas Nagel has criticized Rawls on the ground that decisions reached in the original position are not neutral with respect to all conceptions of the good. The 'primary goods', a fair distribution of which is required by the principles chosen in the original position, 'are not equally valuable in pursuit of all conceptions of the good'. Thus, what may seem agreeable to those in the original position may not be mutually acceptable to actual people in an actual society. (See 'Rawls on Justice', *Philosophical Review*, LXXXII, 2 (April 1973), 228.) Rawls agrees that his theory incorporates a certain ideal of the person and is not neutral among different persons with different conceptions of the good. He argues, however, that no theory is completely neutral in these respects. (Rawls, 'Fairness to Goodness', *Philosophical Review*, LXXXIV, No. 4 (October 1975), Sec. VI esp. p. 549.) If this is so, then it would seem that morality, conceived as a kind of public consensus, will be possible only to the extent that some people are willing either to alter their conceptions of the good or, at least, to treat some of their interests as not constituting a valid claim on others. (For

some further remarks on this point, see the discussion of economic theories later in this chapter.)

12 Roger Wertheimer, *The Significance of Sense* (Ithaca, New York, 1972, Cornell University Press), Ch. III.

13 *Ibid.* The definition of 'ought' is on page 109. I suspect Wertheimer would not accept the account of adequacy I offer here. See his Chapter IV.

14 For the distinction between *proof* and *justification* I have in mind, see Rawls, *A Theory of Justice*, Sec. 87, esp. 580-1.

15 Philippa Foot, 'Morality as a System of Hypothetical Imperatives', *Philosophical Review*, LXXXI, No. 3 (July 1972), 314. The argument in the text relies heavily on Mrs Foot's work, especially on the concluding pages of her 'Moral Beliefs', *Proceedings of the Aristotelian Society*, 58 (1958-9). See also Rawls, *A Theory of Justice, op. cit.*, Sec. 86.

16 One person's belief that others comply with the rules does not, in itself, necessarily give that person a reason to comply himself. For some people, at least, complying with the rules, by itself, is not a convention in David Lewis's sense of the term. (See 'Languages, Language and Grammar' in G. Harman (ed.), *On Noam Chomsky: Critical Essays* (New York, 1974, Doubleday), 255.) Conformity to some moral rules is unstable, at least among some people: while each benefits if everyone complies, universal conformity is not necessary. (See the references in Note 7 above, together with the accompanying text.) But, it may well be true, in most groups, that, if each complies with *and* professes belief in the rules, each thereby has reason to profess belief in *and* comply with the rules. This conjunctive regularity may come to have the status of a convention.

17 I shall rely here on the Bobbs-Merrill edition (Indianapolis and New York, 1958). References in the text to Mill are to this volume.

18 See, for example, Benn and Peters, *The Principles of Political Thought* (New York, Free Press, 1965), 414ff; and Carl Cohen, *Democracy* (Athens, Ga., University of Georgia Press, 1971), Section 14.3.

19 Compare Rawls, *A Theory of Justice, op. cit.*, 'Justice as fairness begins with the idea that where common principles are necessary and to everyone's advantage, they are to be worked out from the viewpoint of a suitably defined initial situation of equality . . . the constitutional process should preserve the equal representation of the original position to the degree that this is feasible' (221-2).

20 See Robert Dahl, *After the Revolution* (New Haven and London, Yale University Press, 1970) and 'Democracy and the Chinese Boxes' in H. Kariel, ed., *Frontiers of Democratic Theory* (New York, Random House, 1970).

21 Benn and Peters, *op. cit.*, 416.

22 Some writers, it seems to me, are excessively concerned about this prospect and hold that moralizing or ideological tendencies should be resisted in favor of the politics of compromise among (mere)

interest groups. At least, this is the impression I get from S. M. Lipset, 'The Paradox of American Politics', *The Public Interest*, 41 (Fall 1975).

23 For discussion of this idea, see Albert Hirschman, *Exit, Voice and Loyalty* (Cambridge, Mass., Harvard University Press, 1970).

24 Jack Walker, 'A Critique of the Elitist Theory of Democracy', reprinted as 'Normative Consequences of "Democratic" Theory' in Henry Kariel, ed., *Frontiers of Democratic Theory* (New York, Random House, 1970), 227.

25 Carole Pateman, *Participation and Democratic Theory* (Cambridge, Cambridge University Press, 1970), V.

26 Here I adopt one of the alternatives suggested by Scanlon in 'Preference and Urgency', *Journal of Philosophy*, LXXII, No. 19 (November 6 1975), 668. The standard of urgency in a morality, he suggests, might not correspond to an actual consensus on what is important and what is not, but might be 'the best available standard of justification that is mutually acceptable to people whose preferences diverge'. For why a standard based on subjective intensity is not likely to work, see Scanlon, 659 and Rawls, 'Fairness to Goodness', *op. cit.*, Section VII.

27 Anthony Downs, *An Economic Theory of Democracy* (New York, Harper & Row, 1957), Ch. 9.

28 S. M. Lipset, *Political Man* (New York, Doubleday, 1960); R. Dahl, *Pluralist Democracy in the United States* (Chicago, Rand McNally, 1967).

VII LAW AND MORALITY:
THE PROBLEM OF POLITICAL OBLIGATION

1 For an example of the kind of abuse I have in mind, see the three part article by Richard Harris, 'The Liberty of Every Man', in *New Yorker*, November 3, 10 and 17, 1975.

2 Philippa Foot, 'Euthanasia', *Philosophy and Public Affairs*, 6, No. 2 (Winter 1977), 85-112.

3 *Ibid.*, 110.

4 For a commonplace example of similar legislative reasoning consider laws prohibiting glass containers on a public beach. There is nothing intrinsically wrong with taking a bottle of pop to the beach. Moreover, any risks involved are negligible in the case of anyone who can be trusted to clean up his trash. The trouble is that people cannot be trusted, and we cannot enforce a law requiring people to pick up their broken glass as well as we can enforce a law requiring no glass at all. (For another commonplace, but far more controversial, example, consider affirmative action requirements that impose some kind of quota. *Perhaps* what is required here is not morally required — or is prohibited — but nevertheless represents the only enforceable means of preventing immoral discrimination.)

The kind of practical considerations that underlie such laws also apply in the controversial case of so-called laws of strict liability making conduct punishable even without *mens rea*. These cases, in turn, are *somewhat* analogous to laws punishing negligent conduct. See Richard Wasserstrom, 'Strict Liability in the Criminal Law', *Stanford Law Review*, 12 (1959-60), 731-45.

5   For discussions of privacy and freedom of expression in these terms see Thomas Scanlon, 'A Theory of Freedom of Expression', *Philosophy and Public Affairs*, 1, No. 2 (Winter 1972), 204-26; and 'Thomson on Privacy', *Philosophy and Public Affairs*, 4, No. 4 (Summer 1975), 315-22.

6   Scanlon, 'A Theory of Freedom of Expression', *op. cit.*

7   Rolf Sartorius, *Individual Conduct and Social Norms* (Encino and Belmont, Ca., Dickenson, 1975).

8   *Ibid.*, 13ff.

9   *Ibid.*, 73ff.

10 *Ibid.*, 56ff.

11 See Ronald Dworkin, *Taking Rights Seriously* (Cambridge, Mass., Harvard University Press, 1977), especially Ch. 2, sec. 5.

12 Gerald Dworkin, 'Non-neutral Principles', *Journal of Philosophy*, LXXI, No. 14 (August 15 1974), 500.

13 See Sartorius's interpretation of Mill's *On Liberty* in Sartorius, *op. cit.*, Ch. 8.

14 Ronald Dworkin, *op. cit.* For additional discussion of the issues concerning me, see Sartorius, *op. cit.*, Ch. 10. On the relation between these issues and the problem of political obligation, see Conrad D. Johnson, 'Moral and Legal Obligation', *Journal of Philosophy*, LXXII, No. 12 (June 19 1975), 315-33.

15 The two alternatives discussed here were brought to my attention by John Troyer's paper 'Does Utilitarianism Tell Us What To Do?' read at the Western Division Meetings of the APA in 1976. I am grateful to John for sending me a copy of his paper.

16 See Allan Gibbard, 'Rule-utilitarianism: Merely an Illusory Alternative?', *Australian Journal of Philosophy* (August 1965), 211-20.

17 David Lyons has recently offered an interpretation of Mill's *Utilitarianism* according to which, roughly, moral principles are those whose requirements we could justifiably enforce by informal sanctions in light of the general goal of maximizing utility. This comes close to turning Sartorius's theory on its head! His non-moral social and legal rules become the principles of morality while his principle of morality (AU) becomes merely a standard in terms of which moral principles are to be chosen. However, Lyons speculates that, for Mill, the requirements that can be justifiably enforced by informal sanctions will merely overlap with the requirements that can be justifiably enforced by formal (legal) sanctions. Hence, there will still be legal requirements that do not correspond to moral requirements. See 'Mill's Theory of Morality', *Nous*, X, No. 2 (May 1976), esp. 110.

What I want to emphasize is that anyone whose moral theory has teleological elements — who takes it that moral principles are somehow based on the production of some goods and the prevention of some evils — must think about the question *in what way* principles are *based on* these goals. Are principles directions for infallible people or for fallible people, for people of good will or corrupt people? Are clarity, easy applicability and enforceability considerations? Are they principles that we can reasonably enforce in light of the costs and benefits of enforcement stated in terms of the goals underlying the morality? Though I have expressed my indebtedness to Thomas Scanlon's work at a number of points, and though I tend to accept his notion that a morality is structured around a set of basic goals and interests, I find him vague on the points I have just mentioned. However, it seems to me, the way we conceive the relation between law and morality will depend to a large extent on whether we say that good laws are based on moral goals in the same way in which moral rules are based on these goals.

18 John Rawls, *A Theory of Justice* (Cambridge, Mass., Harvard University Press, 1971), 18-19, 51-2. (Subsequent unidentified references in the text are to this book.)

19 C. D. Broad, 'On the Function of False Hypotheses in Ethics', *International Journal of Ethics*, XXVI (April 1916), 377-97; H. L. A. Hart, 'Are There Any Natural Rights?', *Philosophical Review*, LXIV, No. 2 (April 1955), especially 185.

20 There are exceptions, however, since Rawls thinks civil disobedience is sometimes consistent with the obligations derived from fairness. See *op. cit.*, 55.

21 Rawls, 'Legal Obligation and the Duty of Fair Play' in S. Hook, ed., *Law and Philosophy* (New York, New York University Press, 1964), 10.

22 See R. Nozick, *Anarchy, State and Utopia* (New York, Basic Books, 1974), 90-5; and Jan Narveson, 'An Overlooked Aspect of the Fairness-Utility Controversy', *Journal of Value Inquiry*, VII, No. 2 (Summer 1974), 124-30.

23 See Narveson, *op. cit.*

BIBLIOGRAPHY

Arendt, Hannah, *On Revolution*, Viking, New York, 1963.

Arrow, Kenneth, *Social Choice and Individual Values*, 2nd edn, Wiley, New York, 1963.

Bachrach, Peter, 'Interest, Participation and Democratic Theory', in *Participation in Politics, Nomos XVI*, J. R. Pennock and J. W. Chapman, eds, Lieber-Atherton, New York, 1975, pp. 39-55.

Bachrach, Peter, *The Theory of Democratic Elitism*, Little Brown, Boston, 1967.

Barry, Brian, *Sociologists, Economists and Democracy*, Collier-Macmillan, London, 1970.

Beam, George D., *Usual Politics*, Holt, Rinehart & Winston, New York, 1970.

Benn, S. I. and Peters, R. S., *Principles of Political Thought*, Free Press, Chicago, 1959.

Bentham, Jeremy, *Principles of Morals and Legislation*, Hafner, New York, 1948.

Black, Charles L., Jr, 'Representation in Law and Equity', in *Representation, Nomos X*, J. R. Pennock and J. W. Chapman, eds, Atherton, New York, 1968, pp. 131-43.

Black, Duncan, *The Theory of Committees and Elections*, Cambridge University Press, Cambridge, 1971.

Broad, C. D., 'On the Function of False Hypotheses in Ethics', *International Journal of Ethics*, XXVI (April 1916), pp. 377-97.

Brown, Stuart M., 'Black on Representation : A Question', *Representation, Nomos X*, J. R. Pennock and J. W. Chapman, eds, Atherton, New York, 1968, pp. 144-9.

Buchanan, James and Tullock, Gordon, *The Calculus of Consent*, University of Michigan Press, Ann Arbor, 1962.

Cohen, Carl, *Democracy*, University of Georgia Press, Athens, Ga., 1971.

Dahl, Robert, *After the Revolution*, Yale University Press, New Haven, 1970.

Bibliography

Dahl, Robert, 'Democracy and the Chinese Boxes', in *Frontiers of Democratic Theory*, H. Kariel, ed., Random House, New York, 1970, pp. 370-93.

Dahl, Robert, 'Further Reflections on "the Elitist Theory of Democracy" ', *American Political Science Review*, LX, No. 2 (June 1966), pp. 296-305.

Dahl, Robert, *Pluralist Democracy in the United States*, Rand McNally, Chicago, 1967.

Dahl, Robert, *A Preface to Democratic Theory*, University of Chicago Press, Chicago, 1956.

Diggs, B. J., 'Practical Representation', *Representation, Nomos X*, J. R. Pennock and J. W. Chapman, eds, Atherton, New York, 1968, pp. 28-37.

Downs, Anthony, *An Economic Theory of Democracy*, Harper & Row, New York, 1957.

Dworkin, Gerald, 'Non-Neutral Principles', *Journal of Philosophy*, LXXI, No. 14 (August 15 1974), pp. 491-506.

Dworkin, Ronald, *Taking Rights Seriously*, Harvard University Press, Cambridge, Mass., 1977.

Foot, Philippa, 'Euthanasia', *Philosophy and Public Affairs*, 6, No. 2 (Winter 1977), pp. 85-112.

Foot, Philippa, 'Moral Beliefs', *Proceedings of the Aristotelian Society*, 58 (1958-9), pp. 83-104.

Foot, Philippa, 'Morality As A System of Hypothetical Imperatives', *Philosophical Review*, LXXXI, No. 3 (July 1972), pp. 305-16.

Gauthier, David, 'Morality and Advantage', *Philosophical Review*, LXXVI, No. 4 (October 1967), pp. 460-75.

Gibbard, Allan, 'Rule-Utilitarianism: Merely An Illusory Alternative?', *Australian Journal of Philosophy*, 43, No. 2 (August 1965), pp. 211-20.

Harman, Gilbert, 'Moral Relativism Defended', *Philosophical Review*, LXXXIV, No. 1 (January 1975), pp. 3-22.

Harman, Gilbert, *The Nature of Morality*, Oxford University Press, New York, 1977.

Harman, Gilbert, 'Relativistic Ethics: Morality as Politics', *Midwest Studies in Philosophy*, III, University of Minnesota, Morris, 1978, pp. 109-21.

Harris, Richard, 'The Liberty of Every Man', *New Yorker* (November 3, 10 and 17, 1975).

Hart, H. L. A., 'Are There Any Natural Rights?', *Philosophical Review*, LXIV, No. 2 (April 1955), pp. 175-91.

Hempel, Carl, 'Empiricist Criteria of Cognitive Significance: Problems and Changes', *Aspects of Scientific Explanation*, Free Press, Chicago, 1956.

Hirschman, Albert, *Exit, Voice and Loyalty*, Harvard University Press, Cambridge, Mass., 1970.

Hobbes, Thomas, *Leviathan*, Bobbs-Merrill, Indianapolis, 1958.

Huntington, Samuel P., 'The Democratic Distemper', *The Public Inter-*

Bibliography

est, No, 41 (Fall 1975), pp. 9-38.

Johnson, Conrad D., 'Moral and Legal Obligation', *Journal of Philosophy*, LXXII, No. 12 (June 19, 1975), pp. 315-33.

Kariel, Henry S., ed., *Frontiers of Democratic Theory*, Random House, New York, 1970.

Keim, Donald W., 'Participation in Contemporary Democratic Theories', *Participation in Politics, Nomos XVI*, J. R. Pennock and J. W. Chapman, eds, Lieber-Atherton, New York, 1975, pp. 1-38.

Kuflik, Arthur, 'Majority Rule Procedure', *Due Process, Nomos XVIII*, J. R. Pennock and J. W. Chapman, eds, New York University Press, New York, 1977, pp. 296-332.

Ladd, John, 'The Ethics of Participation', *Participation in Politics, Nomos XVI*, J. R. Pennock and J. W. Chapman, eds, Lieber-Atherton, New York, 1975, pp. 98-135.

Lewis, David, *Convention*, Harvard University Press, Cambridge, Mass., 1969.

Lipset, S. M., 'The Paradox of American Politics', *The Public Interest*, No. 41 (Fall 1975), pp. 142-65.

Lipset, S. M., *Political Man*, Doubleday, New York, 1960.

Little, I. D. M., 'Social Choice and Individual Values', *Economic Justice*, ed. E. S. Phelps, Penguin Books, Baltimore, 1973, pp. 137-52.

Locke, John, *Second Treatise of Civil Government*, Bobbs-Merrill, Indianapolis, 1952.

Luce, R. D. and H. Raiffa, *Games and Decisions*, Wiley, New York, 1957.

Lyons, David, 'Mill's Theory of Morality', *Nous*, X, No. 2 (May 1976), pp. 101-20.

Mill, John Stuart, *Considerations on Representative Government*, Bobbs-Merrill, Indianapolis and New York, 1958.

Mill, John Stuart, *On Liberty*, Bobbs-Merrill, Indianapolis, 1956.

Nagel, Thomas, 'Rawls on Justice', *Philosophical Review*, LXXXII, No. 2 (April 1973), pp. 220-34.

Narveson, Jan, 'An Overlooked Aspect of the Fairness-Utility Controversy', *Journal of Value Inquiry*, VII, No. 2 (Summer 1974), pp. 124-30.

Nelson, William, 'The Very Idea of Pure Procedural Justice', *Ethics* (forthcoming).

Nozick, Robert, *Anarchy, State and Utopia*, Basic Books, New York, 1974.

Olson, Mancur, 'The Calculus of Consent' (Review), *American Economic Review*, LII, No. 5 (December 1962), pp. 1217-18.

Olson, Mancur, *The Logic of Collective Action*, Harvard University Press, Cambridge, Mass., 1965, 1971.

Pateman, Carole, *Participation and Democratic Theory*, Cambridge University Press, Cambridge, 1970.

Pitkin, Hannah, *The Concept of Representation*, University of California Press, Berkeley, California, 1967.

Plamenatz, John, *Consent, Freedom and Political Obligation*, 2nd ed.,

Bibliography

Oxford University Press, London, 1968.

Rawls, John, 'Fairness to Goodness', *Philosophical Review*, LXXXIV, No. 4 (October 1975), pp. 536-54.

Rawls, John, 'Legal Obligation and the Duty of Fair Play', *Law and Philosophy*, S. Hook, ed., New York University Press, New York, 1964, pp. 3-18.

Rawls, John, *A Theory of Justice*, Harvard University Press, Cambridge, Mass., 1971.

Rousseau, Jean-Jacques, *The Social Contract*, Dutton, New York, 1963.

Sartorius, Rolf, *Individual Conduct and Social Norms*, Dickenson, Encino and Belmont, California, 1975.

Scanlon, Thomas, 'Preference and Urgency', *Journal of Philosophy*, LXXII, No. 19 (November 6 1975), pp. 655-99.

Scanlon, Thomas, 'A Theory of Freedom of Expression', *Philosophy and Public Affairs*, Vol. 1, No. 2, Winter 1972, pp. 204-26.

Scanlon, Thomas, 'Thomson On Privacy', *Philosophy and Public Affairs*, Vol. 4, No. 4, Summer 1975, pp. 315-22.

Schumpeter, Joseph, *Capitalism, Socialism and Democracy*, 3rd ed., Harper & Row, New York, 1950.

Sen, A. K., *Collective Choice and Social Welfare*, Holden Day, San Francisco, 1970.

Simmons, A. John, 'Tacit Consent and Political Obligation', *Philosophy and Public Affairs*, 5, No. 3 (Spring 1976), pp. 274-91.

Singer, Peter, *Democracy and Disobedience*, Oxford University Press, New York, 1973.

Troyer, John, 'Does Utilitarianism Tell Us What To Do?', unpublished typescript.

Walker, Jack, 'Normative Consequences of "Democratic" Theory' (originally 'A Critique of the Elitist Theory of Democracy'), *Frontiers of Democratic Theory*, Henry Kariel, ed., Random House, New York, 1970, pp. 227-47.

Wasserstrom, Richard, 'Strict Liability in the Criminal Law', *Stanford Law Review*, 12 (1959-60), pp. 731-45.

Wertheimer, Roger, *The Significance of Sense*, Cornell University Press, Ithaca, New York, 1972.

Wolff, Robert Paul, *In Defense of Anarchism*, Harper & Row, New York, 1970.

Wollheim, R., 'A Paradox in the Theory of Democracy', *Philosophy, Politics and Society*, 2nd series, P. Laslett and W. G. Runciman, eds, Blackwell, Oxford, 1962, pp. 71-87.

INDEX

International Library of Philosophy

Editor: Ted Honderich

(*Demy 8vo*)

Allen, R.E. (Ed.), **Studies in Plato's Metaphysics** *464 pp. 1965.*
 Plato's 'Euthyphro' and the Earlier Theory of Forms *184 pp. 1970.*
Allen, R.E. and Furley, David J.(Eds.), **Studies in Presocratic Philosophy**
 Vol.1: The Beginnings of Philosophy *326 pp. 1970.*
 Vol. 11: Eleatics and Pluralists *448 pp. 1975.*
Armstrong, D.M., **Perception and the Physical World** *208 pp. 1961.*
 A Materialist Theory of the Mind *376 pp. 1967.*
Bambrough, Renford (Ed.), **New Essays on Plato and Aristotle**
 184 pp. 1965.
Barry, Brian, **Political Argument** *382 pp. 1965.*
Becker, Lawrence C. **On Justifying Moral Judgments** *212 pp. 1973.*
†Blum, Lawrence, **Friendship, Altruism and Morality** *256 pp. 1980.*
Bogen, James, **Wittgenstein's Philosophy of Language** *256 pp. 1972.*
Brentano, Franz, **The Foundation and Construction of Ethics** *398 pp. 1973*
 The Origin of our Knowledge of Right and Wrong *184 pp. 1969.*
 Psychology from an Empirical Standpoint *436 pp. 1973.*
 Sensory and Noetic Consciousness *168 pp. 1981.*
Broad, C.D., **Lectures on Psychical Research** *462 pp. 1962.*
Crombie, I.M., **An Examination of Plato's Doctrine**
 *Vol.1:*Plato on Man and Society *408 pp. 1962.*
 Vol. 11: Plato on Knowledge and Reality *584 pp. 1963.*
Dennett, D.C., **Content and Conciousness** *202 pp. 1969.*
Dretske, Fred I., **Seeing and Knowing** *270 pp. 1969.*
Ducasse, C.J., **Truth, Knowledge and Causation** *264 pp. 1969.*
Fann. K.T. (Ed.), **Symposium on J.L. Austin** *512 pp. 1969.*
Findlay, J.N., **Plato: The Written and Unwritten Doctrines** *498 pp. 1974.*
Flew, Anthony, **Hume's Philosophy of Belief** *296 pp. 1961.*
Glover, Jonathan, **Responsibility** *212 pp. 1970.*
Goldman, Lucien, **The Hidden God** *424 pp. 1964.*
Hamlyn, D.W., **Sensation and Perception** *222 pp. 1961.*
†*Hornsby, Jennifer, **Actions** *152 pp. 1980.*
Husserl, Edmund, **Logical Investigations** *Vol.1: 456 pp. Vol.11: 464 pp..1970.*
Körner, Stephan, **Experience and Theory** *272 pp. 1966.*
*Linsky, Leonard, **Referring** *152 pp. 1967.*
Mackenzie, Brian D., **Behaviourism and the Limits of Scientific Method**
 208 pp. 1977.
†*Mackie, J.L., **Hume's Moral Theory** *176 pp. 1980.*
Merleau-Ponty, M., **Phenomenology of Perception** *488 pp. 1962.*
Naess, Arne, **Scepticism,** *176 pp. 1969.*
†Nelson, William, **On Justifying Democracy** *192 pp. 1980.*
†Newton-Smith, W.H., **The Structure of Time** *276 pp. 1980.*
Perelman, Chaim, **The Idea of Justice and the Problem of Argument**
 224 pp. 1963.
†*Putnam, Hilary, **Meaning and the Moral Sciences** *156 pp.1978.(Paperback
 1980).*
Sayre, Kenneth M., **Cybernetics and the Philosophy of Mind** *280 pp. 1976.*